IMPERIAL AMERICA:
THE INTERNATIONAL POLITICS
OF PRIMACY

Studies in International Affairs Number 2

Studies in International Affairs Number 2

IMPERIAL AMERICA: THE INTERNATIONAL POLITICS OF PRIMACY

by George Liska

The Washington Center of Foreign Policy Research
School of Advanced International Studies
The Johns Hopkins University

The Johns Hopkins Press, Baltimore

Originally published, 1967
Second printing, 1968

FOREWORD

American foreign policy in the first two decades of the cold war has been a striking success, judged by normal standards of national security and power. Even though the world of the mid-1960s bears no resemblance to American ideals of international harmony, the United States has achieved its proximate goal of containing the expansion of Communist control. The moderation of Soviet policy, the loosening up of the Soviet bloc in Eastern Europe, the disruption of the Sino-Soviet alliance, the frustration of Communist China's expansionist ambitions, and the failure of either of the principal Communist states to extend their domains by exploiting revolutions in the backward areas—these developments fulfill the most critical objectives of the policy of containment enunciated twenty years ago. The United States is now clearly the most powerful state in the world by any criterion; it is the only truly global power.

Therefore, it seems likely that American foreign policy in the next decade or so will be concerned less with the problems of assuring containment and more with the problems of fostering a tolerable order in an international environment transformed by the very success of containment and by the great magnitude and scope of American power. In a sense the position of the United States is analogous to that of an imperial, though nonimperialistic, power. In a global domain of power without rule, the United States must exercise its immense influence on a scale of effort and involvement appropriate to its increasingly limited capacity for direct control and compatible with the nation's particular political genius.

From the perspective of America's imperial position, Mr. Liska's penetrating essay examines salient trends in international politics and their implications for American foreign policy. His analytical interpretation is part of the Washington Center's continuing effort to assess and reassess the foundations of American foreign policy in a changing international environment.

This is the second publication in the Washington Center's new booklet series, "Studies in International Affairs."

ROBERT E. OSGOOD
Director,
Washington Center of
Foreign Policy Research

The salient event of American and world politics as this essay goes into print—but not the essay's principal subject—is the conflict in Vietnam. The American commitment in Vietnam may be examined from three major aspects: of strategic options (escalation vs. de-escalation); of its basic rationale (containment of Red China, defense of American security, protection of the South Vietnamese, reassurance of Asian allies); and of the way in which it is being presented to the American people and the world at large.

All three aspects are represented in a conception of the Vietnamese war as the first imperial war the United States has been called upon to fight in the newly emerging constellation of world power and order. The new constellation is basically one of the United States as the manifestly preponderant world power lifted into the new position as gradually and imperceptibly by the falling into place of the Soviet challenge and exertions as it had been dramatically projected into the cold war by the defeat of the Axis. The second component of the new constellation is the emergence of relatively independent—or potentially or would-be independent—centers of policy if not necessarily power in the world at large. In combination with the postcolonial climate and the existence of regional imperialisms the new forces make central co-ordination necessary, while precluding the American responsibilities from being explicitly formulated and exercised at all times and in all situations. The third component is of course the non-existence of an effective organization that could take the place of leadership by a strong state or a combination of strong states.

To sum up, in an unorganized world of conflicting and successive local and regional imperialisms, the United States faces the imperial tasks of maintaining minimum order; in the discharge of these tasks its methods may or must be often indirect (acting through relatively, ostensibly, or up to a point really independent local friendly powers, within limits set by the possibility of a real divergence of their own and American interests) as well as nonprovocative or even nondramatic abroad and at home.

In this perspective the Vietnamese war has been vulnerable to attack if and as long as conducted and presented as a campaign for the independence of a people or for the containment of a particular great power in a second and presumably last stage of containment of world communism which if "won" will have discouraged aggression in the future and permit the United States to go on building in peace the great society of social and racial harmony. Part of this approach has been a premature and undiscriminating, dramatic and even theatrical, search for peace by negotiations against the background of a determined and even ruthless conduct of the war on the battlefield, overheated economy and political dissent at home, and world-wide distaste not so much with American actions as with the administration's real or suspected hypocrisy.

The Vietnamese war will eventually have to be justified and understood instead as one of the less agreeable manifestations of the American world role. This role implies the necessity to define—by force if necessary—the terms on which regional balances of power are evolved and American access to individual regions is secured even as these regions move toward greater self-dependence. In this perspective the war no longer appears a unique event on the favorable conclusion of which all the rest is made to hinge; it becomes in effect and more so than the Korean war a police operation, which may well have to be repeated in comparable situations until such time as a global organism or another global power can take over the task.

In order to be exercised most of the time by indirection and circumscribed delegation, American leadership must on occasion be direct and forcible. But—and this is a vital corollary to any doctrine of leadership—the police operation must be conducted so as to disturb in the least feasible measure both the imperial body politic and the world at large—the automatic critics and adversaries excepted. This can be done so long as the strategy of the war observes the principle of scale—adjusting military means and political propaganda regarding both war and peace to local stakes and resources rather than to the military and diplomatic resources of the United States as a great power, even if this means doing no more than thwart the adversary indefinitely rather than defeating him for good. Such an approach ought to be more feasible militarily and psychologically in a perspective of recurrent police actions (rather than of one more "last" war) and with a political-military establishment that derives from its professionalism a high level of efficiency as well as a moderate measure of detachment. Had it been less dramatized, the Vietnamese war would have been an ideal ground for evolving, training, and breaking in such a combined political-military establishment as well as for educating the American people to changing facts of life. It may still prove retrospectively to have been such, despite the eagerness of administration spokesmen to placate critics (while confusing the public) on

the plane of doctrine, by denying any universal polic-
ing and thus by implication imperial purpose, so as to
be somewhat freer to act in one particular situation of
fact.

The ensuing discussion seeks to place the war in
Vietnam and the political crisis of transition in Europe
in the broadest possible perspective. The essay ana-
lyzes the general problems of empire and imperial
politics and moves gradually to the discussion of contemporary issues. Bibliographical references are limited, with emphasis on historical sources and the author's own past publications which can serve as background or supplement to what follows.

CONTENTS

IMPERIAL AMERICA:
THE INTERNATIONAL POLITICS
OF PRIMACY

Studies in International Affairs Number 2

I. THE SETTING DEFINED: THE COLD WAR AND AFTER

Contemporary international politics is a compound of two ingredients: the politics of reviving or reasserted nation-states and the politics of empire and interempire relations. Imperial politics are tempting but not helpful to discuss, arraign, and dismiss as "imperialistic" in the modern, doctrinaire, and—lately—propagandistic sense of the term. The difference between interstate and imperial or interempire politics is elusive, but to affirm it compels one to go beyond the European state system for antecedents and models, a procedure which if not original is still sufficiently uncommon to justify itself even if it does not produce startling new insights.

After defining the contemporary setting we shall reach back into the remote historical past in search of elements for general propositions about empire and imperial politics; these latter will subsequently be applied to the issues facing the United States in Europe and in Afro-Asia in a discussion that grows less historical and more contemporaneous and even futuristic as it unfolds.

In our time the issue of empire has been brought to the fore by three interconnected events. One is the revolt in both halves of Europe against the imperial sway of the two superpowers, as a result of the declining prospect of a major war between them. Another event has been the apparent decline of the Soviet Union relative to the United States in the mid-1960s, or at least the failure of the Soviets to move manifestly toward "catching up" with America in terms of the fundamental, organic (as contrasted with the military-strategic) components of power. This apparent, and not necessarily definitive, backsliding of the Soviet Union has coincided with its being replaced by Communist China as the chief, or most vocal and conspicuous, challenger to American predominance. The third aspect has been the war in Vietnam, insofar as it is not so much one more anti-Communist campaign but the first imperial war of the United States, fought at the remote frontier of empire with the historically requisite resource of mobility and initiative and dictated by the concern for upholding minimum world order globally while raising issues of virtually direct rule locally and of the implications of a peripheral police action nationally.

The virtually simultaneous emergence of the United States as the primary world power and its immersion in a local war in Asia, conjointly with the growing fluidity in Europe, mark a change in the established pattern and practices of the two postwar decades. The last twenty years have been taken up by a semi-ideological cold war within a pseudonational state system. The cold war rested on the antagonism between two superpowers contesting the succession to the European powers and state system—an antagonism that was intensified but far from caused by ideological differences. To the extent that succession crises—dynastic or other—have always been virtually impossible to avert among states, the cold war was a virtually inevitable consequence of World War II; it requires greater ingenuity to show convincingly how it could have been avoided than to purport to show whose individual errors or terrors had apparently brought it about. Being in part a simulated war substitute, the cold war depended for its plausibility in the longer run on parity—present or anticipated, real or enacted—between the contestants. This was all the more so because, barring parity, the ostensible defender was manifestly stronger than the conspicuous expansionist.

As a quasiwar between quasi-equal powers, the cold war took place within a nation-state system that shared with the dominant conflict a certain air of simulation and, in regard to the new states, anticipation, while serving as the official institutional framework of policy in forums such as the United Nations, the adversary alliance systems, and the transient organizations of the nonaligned countries. The obvious modifier of nation-statehood was the superpower bipolarity itself which, loose or tight, emptied of significant content both the fact of multiplicity and the value of the national independence of the remaining actors in the international arena. Another source of unreality was the uncertain and fluctuating balance between apparently irreversibly declining (if in some instances die-hard) old nation-states and the likewise apparently irresistibly rising new nation-states; the former seemed no longer and the latter not yet in a position to serve as more than objects of superpower competition, not least when erected as fictitious subjects of action for purposes of superpower strategies.

In the two decades following World War II (though to unequal degrees as time went on) the relations between the two superpowers were more specifically governed by three features or aspects which, while bearing on crucial givens of our time, also point to the future and have significant precedents in the past.

The first aspect bears on nationalism in its traditional, and even more in its contemporary anticolonial, expression. In this respect the two more-than-nation-

states fought, at least initially, a contest over which
would have the power to prevent the re-creation of a
war-prone, competitive internation system of the classic
variety. In the end they produced the very result that
each of the combatants had sought individually to
avert in the interest of its preferred alternative; this
they accomplished by means of the generative dynamic
of any protracted two-power contest. At the beginning
of the European state system—which, like the present
global one, was initially saturated by ideological factors—the contest over foremost authority between two
more-than-secular powers, the Empire and the Papacy,
had a similar stake and a similar outcome: the contest
defeated its purpose by conducing directly to the gen-
eration or promotion of powers both secular and several.

The second aspect bears on the emergence of in-
dustrialism as a social value and source of economic
values transcending any nonpragmatic ideology and de-
laying the perception of anything like a hegemonial
threat from the United States to the national independence of the revived or newly created members of
the international system. The delay has been due
not only to the more overt threat from the Soviet
Union but also to the very "legitimacy" of the bases
of American preponderance. This preponderance has
rested principally not on massive military resources or
on marvels of political subtlety, but on economic assets
and industrial potential, which were traditionally ex-
empt from the purview of the balance of power. In our
time they were additionally legitimized by the universality of the desire to share in them and the knowledge
that they would be shared only with American assistance on the part of those who would or should otherwise have been alarmed at their concentration in one

nation. Only as the superiority of the total massive weight of the United States over the restlessly mobile energy of the Soviet Union became incontrovertibly manifest toward the end of the Khrushchev era could the thrust of antihegemonial fears and of containment efforts begin to be redirected from the Soviet Union to the United States. A similar problem was posed, in a crucial period of the European state system, by the coexistence of two threats: a conspicuous one from the traditionally suspect expansionism of France and another from the aggregate power of the empire of Charles V, which was based on the supremely legitimate factors of dynastic inheritance and the medieval ideal of universal order and was thus initially immune to collective counteraction. Only when lapse of time and a dramatic military triumph of Charles V revealed the real balance of power as favoring the Emperor did a shift in the thrust of containment come about and override old and new religio-ideological differences. The international system moved toward a higher state of evolution as a result.

The third and final aspect that governed the relations of the two superpowers is the over-all tendency toward stability between them in the strategic-nuclear field. That stability has rested on reciprocal capacity for crippling though perhaps uneven destruction, regardless of which power struck first. Within these limits the United States regained a quantitative and qualitative advantage in the mid-1960s which, thanks to American military deployment and experience in Vietnam, has not been confined to the nuclear field. Nor is this advantage likely to be significantly reduced by any foreseeable Soviet deployment of antimissile defenses in the late 1960s. However, the Soviet deployment is apt to reinforce a bias endemic in nuclear weapons and their political usability. By and large, nuclear weapons and superiority in such weapons, unless overwhelming, are useful mainly for deterrence of a major attack and for defense of prestige in the face of offensive political initiatives. To the extent that this is true, the new weaponry updates past situations of relatively stable, if competitive, coexistence among powers (such as Venice, the Ottoman Empire, the Holy Roman Empire and later the Germanic Confederation, and even, intermittently, France) that were impregnable in defense but incapable of militarily decisive offense against one another; this kind of situation, incidentally, has been much more common historically than its obverse in the late nineteenth and early twentieth centuries. A well-managed nuclear diffusion, confined to major industrial powers, might further generalize the not-so-unfavorable state of things, while modifying the bipolar character of nuclear international politics. In either event, however, the bias toward stalemate implicit in nuclear weaponry will continue to enhance the crucial significance of economic-industrial capability and of the capacity to secure widespread approval for one's political role—both of which factors have so far favored the United States over the Soviet Union and placed it in a predominant position reminiscent of empire.

II. EMPIRE AND IMPERIAL POLITICS: IN THE PAST AND IN THEORY

So far we have merely asserted that the international system which prevails and is apt to prevail in the foreseeable future has, in addition to its state-system dimension, an imperial dimension. In order to substantiate somewhat that contention we must look, however briefly and selectively, at a more or less remote past which was characterized by empire and by relations between empires and between empires and lesser powers. Before doing so we shall define the identity of "empire" as well as the difference between an interstate system and an imperial system. Against this background we shall then resume the discussion of contemporary issues in later sections.

I propose to use the word "empire" with reference to the historic superstates rather than to the colonial aggregations of more recent times, on the assumption that the former in general and the Roman Empire in particular have more relevance for contemporary American policy than the latter. An "empire" is a state exceeding other states in size, scope, salience, and sense of task. In size of territory and of material resources, an imperial state is substantially larger than the mean or norm prevailing in the existing system. The scope of its interests and involvements is coterminous with the boundaries of the system itself, rather than with a narrower security zone or habitat; the involvement is implemented directly, or else indirectly through client states. The salience of an imperial state consists in the fact that no other state can ignore it and that all other states—consciously or half-consciously, gladly or reluctantly—assess their position, role, and prospects more in relation to it than to closer neighbors or to local conflicts. Finally, the sense of task which distinguishes the imperial state is typically that of creating, and then maintaining, a world order the conditions and principles of which would harmonize the particular interests of the imperial state with the interests of the commonweal. The sense of universal task, related to world order, comes to prevail over the original national or ethnic basis of the empire-founding community, even as strictly defensive national interest and security cease to be distinguishable from the larger concern and order. To sum up, an empire or imperial state is, in the above sequence, a state that combines the characteristics of a great power, which, being a world power and a globally paramount state, becomes automatically a power primarily responsible for shaping and maintaining a necessary modicum of world order. One attribute follows from another, and the last, which merges with function, is the ultimately distinguishing one.

Even more than the difference between a mere great power and an empire, the differences between interstate and empire-centered or interempire relations are those of nuance, not of kind. Where the interstate system is structured first of all by relatively stable relationships reflecting the dominant conflict or conflicts, the key structural feature of the imperial system is the identity and location of the dominant or leading power engaged in shifting conflicts with successive challengers and rivals. Thus where the role and status of individual member states in the first system are defined by their relation to the dominant conflict—as direct parties to it or only as indirect and secondary parties by way of involvement in local conflicts related to the dominant one by the play of alignments—the role and status of states in the second, imperial system are defined by their relationship to the dominant power—as preferential or secondary allies, primary or occasional rivals, and the like. Second, the interstate system is managed typically by military alliances and by militarily supported negotiations as the principal methods for enacting and resolving conflict, pending the supersession of a dominant conflict by the next one. The imperial system is likewise managed by means of alliances, but as much or more as instrumentalities of control as of conflict. Moreover, the imperial system depends largely on fluctuating internal balances of support for, or resistance to, expansion of commitments and controls on the part of influential and vocal elements in the imperial body politic. Third, and finally, the basic transformations from within the interstate system (as distinct from transformation by forces and factors originating outside the international system proper) are due to the (usually) rare shifts from one major and thus protracted conflict to another, concurrent with changes in the ranking of major powers and the intensity of their involvement in interstate relations. By contrast, the main changes constituting transformation in an imperial system are two: a minor one, in the identity of the prime resister to or challenger of the dominant power; and a major one, the decline and disappearance of the primary power as a result of organic developments within such a power which reflect unfavorable trends in respect of usable surpluses and manageable functions within and without. It must also be understood that unlike dominant conflicts in a multistate system, a dominant power is not necessarily replaced or superseded by another, but may yield to an interstate system without a pre-eminent center or to chaos and an interim of troubles.

Even a cursory inquiry into the little we know about imperial policy makers and relations between empires in ancient times brings out the determining importance of vastness of size and of resources; amorphousness or incoherence in structure and inner working; and a tendency to absolute solutions in interempire relations that are themselves characterized by great distance and a certain weakness of constraints that the over-all system will exert on the massive actors. In all these respects, empires and interempire relations differ in their relations and attitudes from compact, coherent, and contiguous states of moderate size and resource, subject to systemic constraints. Such constraints on such states are commonly rooted in the narrowness of the margin of safety or in the meagerness of surpluses available for expansion or other form of aggrandizement in a system in which, typically, the weight of potentially adversary states exceeds that of any one single state.

The distance that usually separates empires is not only geographical but also psychological. It commonly resides in mutual ignorance, including misassessment of power and objectives. Ignorance and misassessment increase with cultural or ideological differences, such as existed between, say, the Egyptian and the Hatti empires prior to the thirteenth century B.C., the Roman and the Parthian (Persian) empires in the first century A.D., the Habsburg and the Ottoman empires in the sixteenth century, and between Britain and Russia in the seventeenth century. If the Romans tended perhaps to underestimate the Parthians, the successive powers of the West tended to behave more like the Greeks facing Persia and to overestimate the offensive power (and "Byzantine" subtlety) of a succession of their Eastern counterparts. Ideocultural differences were not the only factors impeding communication and comprehension; so did the existence of intermediate geographical zones of graduated control and insulation (such as the Armenian buffer, for example, between Rome and the Parthian Empire and subsequently between Byzantium and Islam) and the activities of self-seeking commercial and political intermediaries (such as, in antiquity, the Arabs, Phoenicians, and Greeks).

The fact of "distance" would seem to promote both the attraction of one or another absolute solution and its ultimate defeat. The factors in relations between empires which militated against the unceasing exertions of competitive coexistence—the daily toil of contiguous states—comprised more than the claims to universal sway typical of empire. They also included actual instability of overinflated power structures and the tendency for the relevant political environment to be operationally represented by one rising competitor for universal dominion, rather than by a number of powers available for *ad hoc* alignments in function of changing interests, issues, and conflicts. The "absolute solutions" referred to above are typically those of conquest or isolation and, if both withdrawal and conquest prove unfeasible or undesirable in the face of a common third enemy, condominium. It is an interesting accident that the first relatively detailed historical information on interempire policy in antiquity is the record of protracted warfare between Egypt and Hatti, ending in a condominial alliance as a means for checking the rise of Assyria; the key battle occurred in 1294 B.C. and the basic treaty was signed in 1278. There were later combinations of actual or attempted conquests and condominia between the Babylonians and the Medes, the Romans and the Macedonians (in Illyria), and, more recently, the Habsburgs and the Ottomans in the Balkans (by way of tributary payments and two-faced satellites). Nor were Napoleon and Hitler impervious to the lure of the condominial formula, at least as a temporary device, with respect to Czarist and then to Stalinist Russia.

If conquest occasionally succeeds, condominium does rarely or never, for any length of time. The first recorded, between Egypt and Hatti, held longest—fifty years—largely because of the long rule of the Egyptian Pharoah who initiated it. Commonly, a condominial arrangement fails over the impossibility lastingly to pool functions while differentiating them and to divide territorial spheres of preponderant influence while coordinating them. A pertinent early example is the short-lived condominial arrangement between the Babylonian and Medan empires in the seventh century B.C., which broke up when commercial Babylon set out to become a military empire as well and the hitherto exclusively warlike Medes moved toward the Black Sea in search of commercial outlets. Similarly, Napoleon and Alexander proved unable to resolve in a mutually satisfying way the questions of who, and in what way and proportion, was to control Poland, patronize Prussia, and first combat and then inherit the spoils of the British empire. Since it is inspired by both reciprocal and shared security fears and suspicions rather than by concord, a condominial agreement must be complete between two powers before it can be implemented even halfheartedly against a third; it reverts to intensified hostility at the slightest suspicion of foul play or infidelity. Moreover, agreements to divide and partition —always difficult—will be virtually impossible to perpetuate between empires for which universality of dominion and function are a necessity and a vocation.

Another obstacle to sustained interempire co-operation (as well as to a systemically meaningful enactment of interempire conflict) has been the laggardness of the balance of power mechanism between such superstates. The Egyptian-Hatti condominial alliance, for instance, collapsed when it failed to secure Egypt's assistance for the weaker Hatti empire's intervention against Assyrian encroachments. Flouting of the most elementary dictates of the balance of power by other imperial states served the Romans even more conclusively: the Seleucids of Asia failed to support Macedon on two occasions, and on one crucial occasion (around 200 B.C.) Macedon failed to assist Asia against Rome's intervention in East Mediterranean politics, which comprised an attempt by the two Eastern empires to establish a kind of condominium over the third, Egypt. In whatever other respect the British may have come finally to resemble the Romans, they certainly enjoyed the fruits of a like failure of the balance of power to operate with respect to the colonial empires. That failure disgusted and then defeated first the French and subsequently the Germans, just as the impossibility of dividing or sharing overseas empire had previously proved the undoing of the Dutch faced with rising England.

If the preference for conquest is a function of universalism, the ever-present inclination to withdraw from intense interaction with other states appears to be an expression of the empire's vastness. Failure to act in terms of the balance of power reflects universal aspiration of empire on one level—the level of incompatibility between pre-eminence and balance—and its vastness on another level—that of compatibility between serious setback and survival (including the apparent possibility of matching increments of strength on the part of the adversary in one arena by enlargements at remote peripheries of empire or in its depths). Conversely, the attraction of the condominial arrangement partakes on the one hand of preference for an absolute solution (because of its apparent neatness and finality, which seem to insure against temporary weakening or other form of disadvantage) and on the other of the desire for withdrawal from competitive politics, at least as between the parties to such arrangement.

A still more flagrant expression of the readiness to withdraw (as a counterpart of the drive to expand) is the apparent acceptance as final of setbacks and defeats that, objectively considered, are minor or inconclusive. One textbook example is that of the Seleucid Antioch III of Asia. He first sought to exploit Rome's involvement with Macedon by compensatory forays elsewhere (in Asia Minor and Thrace); yet when a subsequent and belated Seleucid attempt to counteract Roman expansion in Greece met with defeat, Antioch accepted and observed severe peace terms, though able to continue the struggle in Asia. It is true that the Seleucid monarch's power and prudence were widely overestimated prior to the battle of Magnesia (189 B.C.). However, such an overestimate is no more sufficient an explanation for the subsequent retreat and the redirection of Seleucid policies than the exaggeration of Ottoman capabilities on the part of the West is a fully satisfactory explanation for *their* retraction following the surprise victory of Spain and allies at Lepanto (1571 A.D.). In both instances, after an *empire oblige* kind of self-assertion, the bested powers accepted the verdict of a real but also no more than symbolic defeat out of a sense of internal weaknesses best known to themselves. The acceptance also reflected the confidence that the loss could best be repaired by redirection of effort to a less exacting theater, perhaps on the assumption that the triumphant adversary would co-operate—as did Spain by turning away from the Eastern Mediterranean to the Atlantic and as did Rome, at least temporarily, by reverting to her obsession with Macedon. In contrast, Russia's refusal in 1812 to conform with Napoleon's expectations by accepting the arbitrament of initial defeats marked her refusal to act either as an Asian empire or like the Austrian Empire. To be sure, as time went on, less than total defeats before Sebastopol and Port Arthur produced abdications and reorientations reminiscent of ancient empires; nevertheless Russia's willingness to defy Napoleon and later Hitler, and to fall back on her vastness, showed that she shared with empires of all kinds a deep psychic sense of reserve in the hinterland—just as she had followed the imperial instinct in trying to avoid collision with both Napoleon and Hitler and organize security through establishing spheres of influence and interempire copartnerships with competitors of equal or greater strength.

A second and third line of defense, implicit in the physical vastness of empire, are a formidable thing, despite the danger of straining resources and thus activating latent internal weaknesses and tensions. A margin of safety permits an unusually great margin of error in general policy making. It is the mark of an imperial state that it makes others move (and commit errors) by standing still, that it remains salient in its mass whereas others sally hither and thither with equilibristic frenzy. Withdrawal and introversion can alleviate temporary weakness or weariness as well as constitute a gesture of complacency—the latter based on a sense of an irreducible core of internal strength and of manageable functions capable of generating external power more surely than sterile international activism. Finally, withdrawal also reflects a sense of safety through distance from competing empires, be it physical or psychological, genuine or artificially created by reciprocal fear, distrust, and respect.

The positive features of imperial power have their obverse sides and adverse aspects, of course. The choice between conquest and condominium in regard to equivalent powers tends to disappear in the inevitability of conflict as condominium proves illusory; as the balance of power survives both the empire's sense of being above balancing and its inferior ability to move nimbly within the power framework; as the comforts of vastness are offset by complexity, cumbrousness, or incoherence (in organizing resources and relating them to policy); and as the recourse to withdrawal and isolation either proves the avenue to lasting passivity and decay or becomes impossible to achieve even temporarily. The impossibility of withdrawing is especially apt to obtain when what started as a necessity—involvement in external relations in response to internal dynamism or to external opportunity or threat—becomes an addiction to leading individuals or groups, if only because what began as a deficiency—that of manpower to carry out the business of empire with ingrained or learned skill—becomes a surplus, expressing a vested interest. Of old, as at present, the game of empire is the most fascinating of sports: the masses provide an audience to applaud success and boo failure, and the imperial elites contend with their counterpart in other countries and their internal counterelites, who use dissent as a circuitous avenue to direction.

The besetting weakness of empire may thus be the pressure to increase territorial sway and intensify control; but there are different forms of both, unevenly conducive to stability. An empire, like any other state, can expand because of a spontaneous drive for sustenance, booty, or other assets located outside its existing boundary of control; it can be driven into expansion from within by factional or other conflict for power; and it can be drawn into expansion by contests among third powers or by contest with another power over a stake located between them. The first, predatory incentive to expansion is forever associated with the Assyrian Empire; Egypt, after an inside debate over the respective merits of a predatory drive southward and a preventive response to interstate contests to the east of her, was drawn into expansion by concern over the disposition of Syria at the hands of alternative candidates for control over that strategically located region; and Rome's expansion encompassed all three types of incentives in no neat succession. Rome was drawn into expansion—initially largely by contest with Carthage over the Messina Straits and subsequently by her response to conflicts and conquests involving the Hellenic system of states and empires in the East; by contests with Macedon over Greece and Illyria; and with Seleucid Asia over Thrace, western Asia Minor, and, secondarily, Greece again. Finally, the resulting buffer zone created new pressures for further expansion vis-à-vis the empire of the Parthians. In addition Rome was driven into expansion west and east by the peculiar rules and dynamic of triumviral contests over internal power. She also expanded or sought to expand in a spontaneous drive for economic and other profit, not least eastward into Asia.

The primarily driving, predatory empire is a manifest threat to world order. The polity driven into expansion from within is apt to have difficulty co-ordinating the demands of internal power struggle with those of external order and balance. Conversely, the empire drawn into expansion by the more or less remote conflicts and ambitions of third states is in principle capable of reconciling a more or less authentic compulsion to expand and a more or less genuinely felt obligation to order and organize. It also has reason to do so. Major and violent changes in an international system are unavoidably directed against the incumbent of major power in the system, just as revolutionary changes in a society cannot but affect the standing of the social elite. Retreat into passivity and retrenchment of commitments are therefore no more meaningful possibilities for a leading state than they are for members of leading social strata—unless, of course, either is prepared to risk a delayed choice between abdication and large-scale repression.

Just as initial failure to intervene in time with limited means for order may subsequently compel a large-scale intervention ending in more or less involuntary expansion, the failure to exercise with consistency and skill the arts of indirect control over the behavior of lesser states—by way of structure of elites and interests—is apt subsequently to compel an intensification of direct controls as the only remaining alternative to abandonment. Management diplomacy with regard to lesser and at least conditionally friendly powers was at all times different from maneuver diplomacy, which characterizes relations between equal and at least potentially antagonistic powers; as a science of treating lesser powers, management diplomacy had been extensively practiced and often misapplied by classic Rome in her ascendancy and was subsequently perfected by

Eastern Rome—Byzantium—in her decline. Rome discovered in her rise to power that strength was no substitute for statesmanship and skill; that the capacity to eliminate adversaries was not the same as the capacity to evolve new modes of order. Interventionism out of desire to save the Greeks from others and from themselves led naturally, in the absence of a clear will to transfer immediate responsibility to local allies and to refuse to become involved in their ambitions and quarrels, to a demoralizing permanent presence; in the absence of a consistent Roman policy clearly marking out the respective spheres of over-all imperial responsibility and local autonomy, an initial system of remote or indirect controls led to the institutionalization of direct and even oppressive control in Greece and elsewhere. The response on the part of lesser powers and allies, even the most favored, was vacillation between overdependence and overassertion and between doing nothing without Rome and creating *faits accomplis* against Rome; a major consequence was division within and between the lesser countries, between those favoring and up to a point practicing a hard policy of self-affirmation and those practicing a pliant policy of submissive co-operation. By contrast, Byzantium in her decline many centuries later discovered that statesmanship was no substitute for strength, at least not permanently. But for a long time her saving ability was to perfect management diplomacy from a position of conspicuous weakness by constantly adjusting forms and degrees of control to varying pressures for independence, if only as a means for countering competitive enticements by other powers.

The arts of survival for an empire past its prime need not be unlike the arts requisite for effective service to a larger order by a state rising simultaneously to empire and maturity. Similarly, the impossibility of measuring up to an exemplar in certain respects does not rule out the possibility of learning from its mistakes in others. There is an economy of control just as there is an economy of force; and a little of either in time (even if it appears too much when compared with nothing) is often the only alternative to a wasteful expenditure later.

III. THE PAST AND PRESENT KINGS: ASPECTS AND FEATURES OF EMPIRE

Some or most historical analogies can be at once far-fetched and helpful in illuminating the too close at hand. Such is the case when the contemporary situation and America's position in international relations are explicitly compared with remote periods and empires generally and with the Roman Empire in particular.

Outward appearance today continues to be that of a bipolar world. Similarly, the bipolarity represented by Rome and Carthage in the Western Mediterranean and by Rome and Macedon (and, when Macedon fell, Seleucid Asia) in the East pre-existed, and distracted attention from, the rising power of Rome as the focus of world order. The unifocal aspect of the international system is represented today by the pre-eminence of the United States among the powers. In a different set of conditions from what could have been imagined, the present is close to substantiating the contention of the pre- and postindependence Americans who held this country to be an empire. Like Rome from the Seven Hills, the United States was driven by the competitive dynamic of particular interests from its parochial base in the thirteen states into continental and overseas expansion before it grew strong enough to be authentically drawn into global commitments of an unmistakably imperial nature. Like Rome's, America's involvements expanded from specific commitments to allies to general commitments to liberties, as currently defined—to the dismay of critics. Like another parochial country projected into world empire, Castile, the United States seemed to depend on a sense of ideological mission for the inner strength to effect a drastic transition from isolation to global involvement. Like Rome, once involved, the United States has found it easier to ward off the overt enemies of liberties than to lead allies and friends in ambiguous situations with an economy of control that breeds respect without giving rise to unmanageable risks; meanwhile the allies themselves were being polarized—by the conflicting attractions of relying on protection and resisting a protectorate—into those assertively professing independence and those making a profession out of dependence. Finally, as in the case of Rome, the menacing existence of an ascendant Eastern Empire—in this case Communist China rather than Arsacid Parthia—together with the inability of friends and allies in vulnerable areas to stand up under the stress, drew the United States to extend its sway eastward at the very moment when the West (in the guise of ancient Gaul) seemed to offer a genuine choice between expansion and retrenchment.

Standing at what may not yet be the peak of its relative power, the United States has built its pre-eminent position with the aid of immemorial instruments of empire. These include the wide diffusion, in friendly and dependent lands, of an American party (the equivalent of Rome's aristocratic party vis-à-vis the populist Macedonian party in Greece); increasingly widespread economic ties converging at the center (and administered more liberally than Rome was usually able to do because of a chronic imbalance of payments); and a military force, superior in both organization and key weapons to any other force in existence and kept superior by (among other things) a careful concern for limiting the diffusion of crucial weapons among friends and foes alike—not fleets and war elephants, but nuclear submarines and missiles. In order to consolidate the American Empire, however, the United States will have to find functional substitutes for certain of the strengths possessed by Rome. Diffusion and local adaptation of American constitutional models may be the equivalent of regional organizations of friendly and dependent powers for the purposes of emperor worship; access to education and career advancement within and outside the American imperial establishment for its individual friends and allies may serve as equivalent of the significant implications of Rome's unified or dual citizenship; and a relatively small, highly professional military establishment, organized for mobile offensive-defensive warfare at more or less remote—and in America's case ever-shifting—imperial frontiers, may become the equivalent of the Roman legion.

The more or less remotely threatening factors of decline are in many a case the inversions of the requirements of strength and order. One persistent threat to empire—including Rome's—is the open frontier whose defense comes to signify a simultaneous expansion of armed forces, multiplication of ultimately unproductive or disastrous schemes of politicomilitary defense, and the decay of public involvement and civic spirit. In Rome's case, the state's plight was progressively deepened by a chronic imbalance of external payments and by the resort internally to economic activity of the entrepreneurial-innovating type as but an avenue to fortune habilitating for political office (before the political scene was dominated first by successful and later by unsuccessful military leaders). In sum, the decline of Rome witnessed interconnected issues that are already perceptible on the horizon of a still-ebullient America. One issue was the value of military professionalization, considering its initial economic cost and possible future political implications; another related issue was the choice between potentially competing claims of military efficacy in the field and the requirements of apparently subtler or safer devices of political warfare—in Rome's case the not-so-successful strategy of settling and civilizing "barbarians" at the most exposed confines of empire; and yet another, and most serious, issue was the imbalance between economic and political overexertion by the state and the underinvolvement of growing segments of the imperial nation. In the last respect it is worth noting that empires as diverse as those of Rome, Spain, the Ottomans, and Britain found it to be a precondition of success to insulate internal consumer economy from the cost of external activities by supporting the latter from extraordinary sources—such as taxes on dependent peoples; tributes; precious metals from overseas; prizes; or, rooted in once-enforced virtual monopoly, invisible exports—as long as overt or disguised plunder was the only available alternative to heightened productivity.

Viewed against this rapidly sketched general background, what are the specific key features that single out the United States as an imperial state planted at the focus of the international system? They are three: One is the tendency for other states to be defined by their relation to the United States; another is the great and growing margin for error in world affairs which guarantees that, barring an act of folly, the United States can do no wrong under the unwritten law of the balance of power; and yet another has been the slow, hesitant, and still-inconclusive movement toward containment aimed at America's supremacy, which was wholly legitimately arrived at and largely beneficently exercised.

In a unifocal international system, the relationship of any one state to the imperial state is operationally more significant for its role and status than is its position in a regional hierarchy and balance or its declaratory stance on matters of global concern. To single out a few salient instances, although the Soviet Union has occupied the role of most serious adversary, like the chastened Macedonia of Philip V she is also the on balance benevolent neutral vis-à-vis the Asiatic challenger of the day. Mao's China would, of course, wish to appear in the posture not of Seleucid Asia but of Parthia (followed by Sassanian Persia), the intrinsically unsubduable key adversary empire against which the essential strength of the Western Empire will exhaust itself in due course. Juxtaposed with the conditional and unconditional adversaries of the leading state have been the typical array of conditional and unconditional allies. Great Britain can be seen as the modern equivalent of Rhodes. Both one-time maritime empires, having called in the superior power of the new world to redress the balance of the old, thereafter utilized unflinching loyalty as the sole remaining means for claiming the new empire's support. Hoping to guide as well as depend, the dwarfed island powers soon discovered—Rhodes in the controversy over Perseus and Britain in that over Suez—that their standing with the principal ally was contingent on careful avoidance of embarrassing initiatives in major issues of world politics. Clinging to a special position for herself, Britain has had to share with West Germany in Europe and Japan—together with such lesser countries as the Philippines, Thailand, and Pakistan—in Asia the standing of preferred ally in a more or less artificially inflated position and with different degrees of regional ambition. In the Roman scheme of things this position, a coveted if strenuous one in each imperial system, was occupied without lasting profit by Pergamum in Asia Minor with respect to weakened Macedon and by Massinissa's Numidia in North Africa with respect to subdued Carthage. The opposite category is that of potentially rebellious friends and allies, dependable only as long as they retain a hard-to-define but easy-to-sense measure of independence and regional influence. Macedon of Perseus, Pontos of Mithridates, the Aetolian League in Greece, come to mind almost as readily in the Roman context as do the France of de Gaulle, the very early United Arab Republic of Nasser, and, as an even more hypothetical possibility, a "Gaullist" Europe in the American system. Finally, there are the uncontrollable and uncommitted tribes and nations—the "barbarians" of Rome's day and the "developing" nations of ours—hopefully biding their time while farming out tokens of amity to the highest bidder.

At all times the most resolute defenders of small-state independence against hegemony were lesser states having themselves a felt imperial past or a present leadership ambition: Athens and Sparta against Persia, Perseus' Macedon against Rome, Venice against France in Italy, and now France against America in Europe. But, with the temporary exception of Athens, whose imperial days lay in the future, these same powers were typically too suspect to the states truly small in size or spirit to serve as rallying points for united action for collective independence. Indeed, if history is a guide, unification or a measure of it is more often than not the handiwork of actors and regions with a relatively modest claim to past or present political or cultural achievement—in the case of Egypt, it was the work of the feudal upper Nile region rather than of the city-states of the lower Nile delta; in Greece, of the rustic Aetolian League rather than of urban Athens or Thebes; in Italy, of Piedmont rather than of Venice or Rome; in Germany, of Prussia rather than of Austria or Frankfurt; and in Europe, of her East rather than her West?

We have also suggested that the United States is an empire because of its great margin for error. This impression may be emerging only progressively and in retrospect, so much was the contrary impression fostered by the hypothetical dangers of the nuclear power and the often exaggerated impression of Soviet ruse as well as power. It is true that, in the mode of the *nouveau riche,* the United States behaved in those areas where economics and politics meet as if there were no limit to what could be done, internationally, with material assets—an attitude shared in their own "foreign aid" policies by gold-rich rulers, from the Pharaohs of Egypt to and beyond Philip II of Spain. Apart from that, however, the alleged "illusion of omnipotence" was indulged in largely or only toward allies, whose power of political resurgence or at least of resentment was discounted, while something closer to an "illusion of impotence" often appeared to govern policies toward overrated adversaries and neutrals. Just as one may endlessly and fruitlessly argue which particular act of omission or commission on the part of the United States or the Allies was "responsible" for the cold war, one may sharpen his wits without cutting through to a demonstrable conclusion by arguing which of a range of particular policies of concession or constraint would have been more or most successful in America's approach toward Eastern Europe, Afro-Asia, the Western Hemisphere, or the Far East. Instead, the fatalistic conclusion is likely to emerge that just as the cold war was inevitable so, once America's power was introduced into a situation, its very weight —levied by act or even failure to act—compelled lesser powers into a series of complicated maneuvers apt to cancel out into something like failure when compared with their original intent.

Whether Tito was bailed out unconditionally in 1948 or was confronted with the prospect of being sucked back into dependence on the Soviet Union if he did not pay for American support with structural changes in the Yugoslav internal system; whether Nasser was backed for a while or blocked right away in his drive for Arab unity under anti-Occidental slogans; whether Stalin and Khrushchev were bluntly or only deviously denied success over Berlin, and Khrushchev faced with a quarantine off Cuba or an invasion in Cuba; whether the United States did not bomb North Vietnam at all, bombed only military targets, or bombed Hanoi massively after a timed ultimatum— these were not alternatives that spelled the difference between conspicuous success and total failure. They were rather, and only, differences in kinds of success and in the timing of different stages in the unfolding of success, as the world subsided into a pattern ever more conformable with America's growing relative power and progressively scaled-down global purpose. As time went on the purpose itself was defined more realistically in function of growing worldly intelligence rather than of a gnawing sense of inadequacy and weakness. The great, and even there not really fatal or irreparable, mistakes were reserved for Western Europe, as the almost always mistimed successive strategies of friendly suasion, direct or devious pressure, and real or simulated disinterest paralleled schemes of merely Continental integration, visions of

Atlantic partnership, and realities of Asian involvement, in function of subsequently belied appearances of military need in Europe, American economic weakness relative to Europe, and European disloyalty to America.

The relationship between Europe and Afro-Asia has been the odd one of disparity in the kind and form of key issues and of reciprocal influence chiefly through the medium of American policy. The oddity has been manifest in regard to the third aspect of America's imperial present: the gathering tide of what might be called countercontainment of the United States under an ambivalent and so far half-hearted Soviet leadership. In the background of this countercontainment has been the erosion of the three main conditions that normally uphold stabilized relationships of rivalry between major powers.

One is the availability of outlets for competition short of acute conflict, which is the alternative to conflicts spilling back from the periphery to the center. Another is the maintenance of rough parity in extant or firmly anticipated material power between the competitors which circumscribes fluctuations due to internal development in the long run and is facilitated by countervailing balance-of-power adjustments (elevating the temporarily weaker and depressing the temporarily stronger power) in the short run. The final condition is habitual adjustment of conflicts in ways and on terms which are not humiliating for any one party—or at least not for the same party all or most of the time. These conditions were for a time really or fictionally present in the American-Soviet relationship, but have been lately passing away rather precipitately. Competitive outlets in the Third World have dried out as stakes proved undefinable and as temporary success for either superpower proved as frustrating and more expensive than immediate failure. The relationship of parity has continued to be enjoyed in the two unreal worlds of the United Nations Security Council and of the nuclear club, although even there in ways susceptible of circumvention by resort to more efficacious means on a lower level and wider basis—be it conventional or subconventional warfare or unconventional, parliamentary diplomacy. In respect of internationally usable economic and military-technological power, the trend has been seemingly away from parity—real or anticipated—toward growing disparity. Soviet thrusts in Berlin, the Congo, and in Cuba were attempts to concretize the conceded or simulated parity before time ran out on a temporary and, as events proved, equally or more fictional superiority in one branch of technology; they produced humiliating defeats and retreats. Soviet unreadiness to oppose with effect American aerial attacks on the territory of a small Communist country has thus been only the latest humiliation in a fairly rapid succession. It is, however, also the first that has presented the Soviet Union with an opportunity to actualize the hitherto latent operation of the short-term, mechanical equalizer between unequal or unevenly developing powers: the balancing of power.

The spill-back of conflict from what only recently was the colonial periphery to the European center cannot today take the eighteenth-century form of an intensified military contest over combined maritime and continental hegemony of any one European state. Instead, the backlash from Asia to Europe has been a highly muted and politicized one. It has been muted by the existence of nuclear weapons, if only in the sense in which these ultimate weapons undergird the largely self-sufficient proximate restraints—restraints that are implicit in the scope of resources that can be practically allocated and of objectives that can be practically pursued in relations between intrinsically saturated industrial states with insatiable consumer publics. This situation has favored low-intensity responses to long-range issues and organizational solutions to structural issues —with the exception of issues surviving from the Stalinist phase into the Maoist era of the cold war and of those aggravated by partition, such as Vietnam today and, not impossibly, Germany tomorrow. Militarily muted, the political backlash is not immaterial. It has presented the Soviet Union with the possibility of translating relative military weakness into relative diplomatic advantage vis-à-vis the United States and of utilizing means other than propaganda in a part of the world relatively immune to Chinese propaganda. The opportunity has its price, however. To be able to use it with effect, the Soviets would have to downgrade not only their ideological commitments but also their nuclear-power solidarity with the United States, in favor of a geopolitically conditioned politicoeconomic solidarity of powers which, in relation to America, are secondary powers.

So far, the limited convergence of Franco-Soviet policies has been the first significant token of a trend toward countercontainment. It has reflected joint interests with respect to the American involvement in Asia on the part of past masters in Indochina and of present allies-enemies of Communist China; the basic common interest, however qualified by differences in peacemaking tactics, has been to minimize the danger of adverse—and to exploit the potentially positive— political and military repercussions of the conflict. More importantly, the rapprochement has reflected convergence of national interests and objectives in Europe. The Soviet Union's substantial interest is in re-consolidating its position in Eastern Europe. This may henceforth be feasible only in a larger European frame-work; if so, all Europe must be shielded as much as possible from American economic penetration and political influence. To this motivation may be added the prestige interest in compensating humiliation in Asia by contributing to an American setback in Europe. The corresponding interest of France is in escaping from one-sided political and technological dependence on the United States. To do so she has been prepared to accept some dependence on the Soviet Union for diplomatic status and scientific technology, in return for some Soviet dependence on French good will in regard to the potentially explosive issues of nuclear evolution in Germany and politicoeconomic evolution in the areas between Germany and Russia. On both the German and the Eastern European counts, the com-munity of interests between France and Great Britain may in the not-so-long run prove stronger than their discordance over the ultimate political purpose of the Franco-Soviet rapprochement—a discordance that may diminish with the next swing in the British foreign policy pendulum from one traditional position, that of leaning on the strongest conservative power, to an-other, that of balancing the power too strong for its own and the general good. Meanwhile, largely ignor-ing an England reminiscent internationally of the sec-ond Tudor rather than of the first Elizabeth, France and Soviet Russia have been re-enacting the partial and ambivalent association between the both stronger and stronger-willed contemporaries of Henry VIII, Francis I and Suleiman the Magnificent. The Franco-Ottoman "alliance" against the Emperor Charles V was long delayed and always hampered by differences in specific objectives even more than in general ideology. It did not go beyond a trading agreement in its form and it did not produce any momentous joint military or political action. But it did initiate the switch of containment from France to the Habsburgs and the rise of the Western emperor's Eastern counterpart to diplomatic respectability. As a result the association affected the international politics of its time more than many a full-fledged alliance.

The pre-eminent position of the United States is responsible for what we have called the unifocal character of the contemporary international system, while the existence of competing imperial power imparts to international politics the special flavor of interempire relations. This does not mean that the present international system does not retain some and may not be regaining further features of a multipolar system. The interpenetration of features is reflected practically in the United States' being a globally primary power that is not—and should not try to be—paramount in each and every particular area or region of the world system. We shall deal with the definitional and general aspects of a mixed international order and then move into European questions by way of discussing Soviet-American relations as an example of interempire relations in the contemporary setting of an international system uncertainly evolving from a bipolar structure to a multipolar structure with a single focus.

An empire-centered (or imperial, or unifocal) international order differs in some key characteristics from order in a multistate system pure and simple, without an imperial focus or center, whether it be bipolar or multipolar. The differences in regard to "order" are comparable in nature to the differences previously outlined in regard to "system." Features that are basic to, and distinctive of, the pure multistate order have merely an ancillary, supporting role in the imperial order. Thus, the key structural guarantee of minimum order in a pure multistate system is the distribution of antagonistic power in a reciprocally countervailing pattern. In a system focused on one foremost imperial state (even if that system comprises more than one state that possesses or seeks to acquire the attributes of empire), the order rests in the last resort on the widely shared presumption of the ultimately controlling power of the imperial state; this is true even if the manifestation of the controlling power is only intermittent, because the countervailing dynamic continues to operate most of the time. Next in importance to the structure and dynamic of power in maintaining minimum order are certain norms of behavior. The principle of reciprocity in the multistate context is compounded in the empire-centered order with the principle of primary responsibility of the imperial state (however much such responsibility may be circumscribed by the duty of receptivity to the viewpoints of lesser states and their ultimate right of revolt against abuses). Finally, the difference lies in the character of typical or feasible individual or collective sanctions for disorderly or deviant behavior. In gross terms, deviancy will be defined in the pure multistate system as consisting of acts aimed directly or indirectly, forcibly or otherwise, at substantial unilateral changes in the status quo—"substantial changes" being construed as changes that more than routinely impair established interests and modify existing ratios of power and influence. In the imperial system, the critical deviant actions are those which, apart from aiming at substantial changes, are also calculated to abridge access by the responsible power to any particular area for purposes of police and protection against unilateral forcible changes, in such a way as to compel resort to a major display of force and authority if access is to be reopened. The present international quest for order displays a compound of multiactor and one-center situations and approaches, producing conflicts and maladjustments as well as a measure of reciprocal reinforcement.

The problem of countervailing and controlling power as the structural basis of order is of greatest significance. In Europe, the residual controlling power of the United States in Western Europe and of the Soviet Union in Eastern Europe continues to implement the checking and balancing policies of the superpowers. A parallelly emerging potential all-European order, however, is implicit in a Franco-Soviet entente with a countervailing intent vis-à-vis the United States as the globally primary power, whose European presence is to be reduced to the lowest level requisite for, and compatible with, the autonomy and equilibrium of a European state system. In Asia, the United States has been exercising a considerable measure of controlling influence while engaging—militarily in Vietnam and politico-diplomatically on a wider front—in a policy of countervailing the Communist Chinese attempt to supplant the United States as the controlling center of a Southeast Asian regional system. In Latin America, the United States has resisted, so far with success, the projection into the hemisphere of countervailing extraregional power in the interest of its paramount control in the region, regardless of whether such countervailing power were to take the form of a revolution in strategic relationships, such as was implicit in the installation of Soviet missiles in Cuba, or of Soviet or Communist Chinese efforts to export or exploit local social revolution. In regard to Africa, finally, the global picture has been that of a balancing of power and influence among several non-African greater powers, controlling pre-eminence of either being localized and fluctuating, while intraregional actors have been simultaneously engaged in attempts to set up co-operative agencies on the widest possible basis and to offset potentially controlling particular aggregations with countervailing ones.

The next problem is that of reciprocity vs. responsibility. Reciprocity can operate between both comparable and greatly unequal powers. As between the powers that are or can plausibly conduct themselves as "world powers," reciprocity has come to bear on access to political, economic, or cultural role and influence in regions where other powers exert or feel entitled to exert primary responsibility and more or less extensive control. This form of reciprocity is especially hard to work out; it is, however, increasingly the hard-core problem of contemporary world order. The issue of access has been raised between the United States and the Soviet Union, in regard to American access to Eastern Europe and Soviet access to either the Caribbean or Western Europe (or both); between the United States and Communist China with regard to Southeast Asia and Africa; between the Soviet Union and Communist China with regard to South Asia and Eastern Europe; and between France and the United States with respect to Latin America and North Africa, largely as a counter in the competition over the distribution of influence in Western Europe herself. Between unequal powers, reciprocity does not mean reciprocal access but reciprocal performance: the *quid pro quo* of "mutual" assistance programs. It has arisen—and by its nature has never been stably settled—between, say, the United Arab Republic on one side and both the United States and the Soviet Union on the other, just as it has between the U.A.R. and the recipients of *its* assistance in Yemen. The issue of reciprocity in the international order has been pertinent more generally, of course, in regard to such matters as intensification or moderation in the nuclear arms race between the two superpowers, activation and deactivation of territorial and other demands in relations among the small new states, and admission of new members of the United Nations—all areas in which the two superpowers have claimed special and on occasion joint responsibility.

Reciprocal concession or denial of access presupposes the paramount responsibility by someone in a particular area. The American tradition of the Monroe Doctrine is that of persistent denial of access by either the reactionary Holy Alliance or an unholy alliance between indigenous sociorevolutionary movements and Soviet or Chinese communism in Guatemala, Cuba, the Dominican Republic, and everywhere else. One consequence of the American attitude has been to reduce the possibility of meaningful bargaining and barter aiming at a "new deal" between the United States and the Soviet Union with regard to Europe and other parts of the world which would go beyond generalized detente and beyond entente on selected nuclear issues only—an inhibition which is a key element favoring an ultimate "European" solution in and for Europe. By contrast, the French and the Soviets seem to be prepared to explore the possibility of combining primary role or responsibility within their respective regions with some reciprocity in sharing leadership and, especially, of shoring up each other's pre-eminence in the factors or areas in which either of them is or may become deficient. The conspicuous asymmetry in their respective power positions would be lessened by reciprocal attribution of individually most-needed assets: diplomatic standing (and technological know-how) for France and diplomatic respectability (and quality consumer goods) for the Soviet Union. Moreover, both powers would consolidate their position in Europe as a precondition to upholding in the longer run their primary responsibility in the extra-European geographic extensions of their immediate habitat: France's in North Africa, both affirmed and subtly undermined by such affairs as Bizerte and Ben Barka; Soviet Russia's in parts of Asia, more deliberately and dramatically threatened by the Chinese Communists than France's position in North Africa is either by the United States or the United Arab Republic and yet inconclusively affected by evolving Soviet attitudes toward conflicts between third powers over Kashmir or the seventeenth parallel.

The war in Vietnam, together with the partly derivative developments in Burma, Indonesia, and Thailand, has raised the issue of who has primary responsibility in Southeast Asia: the United States or Communist China. Aside from its ambiguity as either an anti-Communist crusade or a routine imperial war, the Vietnamese conflict has displayed also the complementary ambiguity about great power objectives. Have the United States and Communist China been asserting the claim to primary responsibility or only the right to access, even though the United States would not presently think of conceding to Communist China reciprocity in access to areas closer to the American homeland and more vital for American security than either Vietnam or Southeast Asia? It is probable that the issue of reciprocity will not arise between the United States and China, except concerning the conduct of the war, as long as Chinese policy continues to be Maoist and Maoism continues to reflect the present theses of Mao. However, the issue of reciprocity may well arise in some form, if only in regard to Southeast Asia, be-

tween the United States as the military victor in Vietnam and the Soviet Union or France as the interested
powers with capacity either to mediate a negotiated
settlement or else guarantee the North Vietnamese
against wider implications of a *de facto* subsidence of
the conflict in circumstances that would leave the
United States in essential control of the military battlefield—even if not necessarily of the entire political
battlefield.

Finally, the Vietnam issue illustrates the issue of the
critical deviance from the basic norm in a pure multistate and an imperial order. For a multistate order, the
critical issue is the attempt to effect unilaterally a forcible change pure and simple; such deviance calls for
corresponding sanctions to be applied against the ostensibly and directly delinquent state. The agency currently entrusted with the task is the one that has so far
in effect disclaimed competence in the Vietnamese
crisis: the United Nations. From the viewpoint of a
one-center, imperial order in present circumstances, the
critical action is the attempt to abridge and even abolish the capacity of the United States to act decisively in
Southeast Asia in the future without having to resort
to an all-out (including nuclear) war or threat of war.
The corresponding sanction is to retaliate in kind
against the competing great power without meticulous
regard for the precise degree of its complicity in the
defiance and to bar its access to the area by way of action directed against either the ostensible, or the suspected real, culprit as a matter of expediency rather
than principle. Similarly, Nasser's nationalization of
Suez was from one viewpoint no more than a unilateral
change with forcible implications, while from another
viewpoint it was mainly an act to inhibit or deny access
to the area by formerly dominant powers, notably in-

sofar as it implied also abridgment or abrogation of the British treaty right to return to the Suez canal zone militarily in an emergency. The consequence of the two aspects of the case was conflict over the nature of even theoretically appropriate sanctions. Similarly, Indonesia's confrontation with Malaysia (and previously with the Netherlands over West New Guinea) was a bid not only for unilateral change but also for substituting local imperial control and responsibility for that of the extraregional center or centers, decreasingly Dutch and British and increasingly American. The nature of appropriate response and sanction would again have been different, depending on which aspect were to be selected as the dominant one, in part because the avowable one in this or that forum and context.

Not all possible threats to world order are ambiguous in the above sense. Somalia's territorial claims on Ethiopia and Kenya, for instance, raise the possibility of unilateral forcible change but not of regional imperial pre-eminence. Moreover, two boundary cases or classes of disorder are not necessarily covered by either case of deviance. One is acute chaos and low-level destruction, such as those occurring in the Congo and in Nigeria in the 1960s. The issue of unilateral change would arise only if the disturbance assumed external implications, for instance by way of the attempt by another state, such as Ghana in the case of the Congo, to exploit the situation for its direct aggrandizement. The issue of access did actually arise in the case of the Congo conjointly with its internationalization, in the form of the Soviet attempt to supplant the Western powers and the United States in particular, presumably as a preliminary to abridging Western access to the area. The attempt backfired in the framework of a

United Nations action ostensibly concerned with other, more conspicuous aspects of the disorder. The success of the United States in asserting at once its global and local-regional primacy over the Soviet Union was tarnished only when it tried, ill-advisedly, to have the Soviets share the costs of their own humiliation.

The other potential source of disorder and high-level destruction, which is in a class by itself, is nuclear diffusion. In principle, acquisition of nuclear weapons constitutes neither a unilateral change of a kind requiring or warranting multilateral sanction, nor does it provide in and by itself a warrant for action in defense of politicoeconomic access to a particular region. In practice, of course, the situation will be different. If nuclear weapons are acquired by countries with exceptional potential for internally disorderly and internationally deviant behavior, the latent sense of joint responsibility for order on the part of the superpowers is apt to be tested as to its being merely, or more than, declaratory and platonic—with momentous consequences for the nature and incumbency of ultimate authority in world affairs. If nuclear power passes into the hands of a major regional power, with potential for shaping a regional order in its image, the equation of countervailing power and the balance of controlling influences from within and outside the region will be changed in any event. But the specific attitude of the United States as the globally primary power in particular is apt to vary depending on the estimate of the point at which and the extent to which its conception of order will differ from that of the local power or powers. Nuclear weapons in the hands of the United Arab Republic is not the same as nuclear weapons in the hands of the United States from any viewpoint. Similarly, the United States—and the Soviet Union—is apt to view in quite a different light the dispersion of nuclear weapons to Japan or India and to Communist China in Asia, just as the Soviet Union—and the United States—is apt to be less upset by a French *force de frappe* than by a West German nuclear *streitmacht* in Europe. An abstractly formulated antiproliferation treaty that slurs over such differences may therefore well prove just as inappropriate and even counterproductive as did all comparable general instruments in the past which failed to differentiate realistically between cases of common disorder while providing guidelines for evasion and incentives for recrimination—often as a prelude to violation or denunciation of the basic treaty.

V.

THE WORLD TODAY AND TOMORROW: INTEREMPIRE AND INTERSTATE RELATIONS

In a system such as the contemporary one, there is no substitute for constant and alert manipulation and adjustment of concrete interests by interacting states. The United States in particular must so act, as the primary global power, alone or in conjunction with the other imperial state or states as they develop the will and capacity to co-operate in the interest of minimum world order. Just as is the pre-eminent position of the United States, so, however, are the relations between the two established imperial states circumscribed presently by the existence of other states constituting a multistate and, to an as yet uncertain degree, a multipolar international system (the difference being that the individual states are not only actors in the irreducible sense of the word but are also subjects of relatively independent power capable of exercising initiatives and assuming responsibilities as well as of influencing the behavior of the two superpowers). This fact will be seen to reduce, but does not wholly abolish, the relevance of historical precedents for the contemporary Soviet-American variety of interempire relations. Such relations, we have noted previously, are conditioned by the vastness of imperial states and the distance between them; by their propensity to favor the absolute solutions of conquest, condominium, or withdrawal from competition; and by their tendency to administer with some ineptness the balance of power, in consequence of their size, pretension to universality, and their prevalence as strong actors over a weak system.

So far, the relations between the United States and the Soviet Union have conformed unevenly to the historically based pattern. The vastness of the two countries and the size of their resources were clearly the basic factors in originating and shaping their interaction—factors the significance of which was augmented rather than depreciated by the simultaneous emergence of long-distance nuclear weaponry. The great psychological distance between the two countries—consisting of as well as reinforcing ignorance and misjudgments of one another's power and, occasionally, purpose— was not solely or even primarily due to differences in ideology; it was also an extension into our time of a constant derangement in the relations of successive empires of the West and the East. The physical distance between the core lands, even if not between the respective foreposts of empire, was abolished by long-range delivery systems for weapons of mass destruction in the two realms of military hardware and abstract strategic speculation. But no amount of emphasis on this revolutionary change could seriously curtail an instinctive sense of reciprocal immunity based on distance, on the part of most people most of the time in American-Soviet relations. As a result, systemic rivalry and ideological antagonism stopped short of felt hostility of the kind that would unavoidably have entered into a comparable rivalry between compact, coherent, and contiguous territorial states. The Soviet-American "war" could remain "cold," not only because of nuclear deterrents but also because it was not a civil war within a single family of culturally and ideologically cognate (Western or Eastern) nations and because it never became a national conflict between territorial neighbors turned historical enemies. In this respect it resembles the conflict between Habsburg and Ottoman much more than the conflicts between Spain and England or France, between France and England or Germany, or between Russia and China. Distance was not the only factor that helped keep the American-Soviet conflict over power, status, and, to a degree, ideology on a relatively low level of intensity even in its most acute stage. Just as in the Habsburg-Ottoman conflict, other factors produced an appearance or expectation of parity in strength which kept fanaticism and desperate recourse out of the formulation of policy and ensured that the underlying similarities in historical experience and evolving concerns would be translated into a sense of limited but still reassuring solidarity. And lastly, even the remaining or developing asymmetries, not least in material resources, came to produce in both instances (Habsburg-Ottoman and American-Soviet) a salutary and stabilizing divergence in the thrust of policy-making concern.

Under the circumstances, attempts by either power to conquer the other were almost entirely ruled out. Initially, such a conquest was considered too costly and, increasingly, undesirable, certainly from the American and lately perhaps also from the Soviet viewpoint. Neither of the superpowers can confidently expect to deal effectively with the vacuum of ordering authority which the disintegration of the other would create or to profit from its elimination from global and regional balances. The imbalances inherited from World War II were to be remedied, not merely reversed and amplified. If conquest was ruled out—definitively or for the time being (which tends to expand)—a near-absolute solution might still be found in second-best substitutes: the nuclear arms race and the economic growth race. Although the two imperial states preferred to confine the nuclear race to themselves or, at worst, to reliable and well-established industrial states, they soon extended the economic race with high hopes into the Third World of undeveloped new states. As the substitutes for war and conquest unfolded, the impossibility of securing a decisive and final advantage in either was revealed. This revelation was, however, offset by their potential for withdrawal and condominium.

In the nuclear field, withdrawal means stress on deterrence and defense, including deployment of land-to-air antimissile missiles, begun by the Soviet Union in 1966. In the field of economic growth, withdrawal spells emphasis on the "construction of socialism" or on Great Society as an alternative to wasteful contest with the other superpower or to a disappointing build-up of third powers as a corollary to such contest. In the case of the Soviet Union, any such withdrawal into at least temporary isolation or redirection of effort to more accessible areas or to less superior adversaries—in Europe toward the politics of countercontainment or in Asia toward military confrontation with China—would not be unprecedented. It would be in keeping with traditional Russian behavior in foreign affairs and in line with the characteristic response of empires generally to less than decisive, but still symtomatic as well as symbolic, defeats—for a second time over Berlin and over Cuba in the second round.

As for condominium, the nuclear arms race has a manifest potential in that respect. It may take the form of steps to impede an unregulated or any dissemination of nuclear weapons in general and to retain the last word in regard to German nuclear rearmament in particular; or if the stress of unprecedented positive danger suddenly created the possibility of pooling functions while maintaining existing spheres of preponderant interests, nuclear condominium might even go further toward *de facto* joint superpower control over the employment of nuclear weapons already in possession of third states.[1]

The economic-growth competition is likewise susceptible of being inflected toward condominium—e.g., by pooling functions in foreign aid so as to reflect special endowments of the two imperial states while maintaining the division of some of the world space into areas of primary responsibility and therefore of influence. So far, condominial elements have been modest, if multiplying: some community of views on the part of the industrial as against the nonindustrial countries in general discussions of economic development; parallel, specific, and unintentionally complementary economic-aid programs in the United Arab Republic and elsewhere, in a political context minimizing the recipient's leeway for playing the donors off against one another; and community of interests in regard to the politicomilitary preconditions of development or sheer survival in areas of acute conflict bordering on China, such as that between India and Pakistan.

A straw in the wind may have been the apparent willingness of the United States to experiment with converting the Organization for Economic Cooperation and Development from a vehicle of containment into that of some kind of economic condominium by associating the states of Eastern Europe with the organization. A condominial role for the OECD would mean exploiting a set of presumed common American-Soviet political interests vis-à-vis Europe—just as the still more tentative idea of pooling managerial and re-

---

[1] See the author's discussion of "adversary" and "co-operative" superpower control in Alden Williams (ed.), *Arms, Science, and Politics* (Columbus, Ohio: forthcoming).

lated know-how among advanced countries of East and West would put to political purposes the affinity of the industrialized superpowers with regard to the less developed countries.[2] The strategy of "bridge-building" or "peaceful engagement" between East and West in Europe—of which the OECD idea is part—aims at creating an alternative to compact ideological and politicomilitary camps; but it would also prevent that alternative from being a loose and potentially conflictual European state system. Such a system might well be subject to all kinds of jockeying for position as a substitute for or preliminary to revived territorial conflicts and would entail a tendency to outflanking alliances with extra-European parties—China against Russia and perhaps one day a disaffected Argentine or Brazil against America—as a means of satisfying individual or collective prestige needs and, even worse, territorial ambitions. In the circumstances the somewhat creaky vehicle of multilateralism might be useful to hold back any one or all of the four horses of an apocalyptic irredenta: that of Germany and of China, the middle kingdoms of Europe and Asia, reclaiming both land and greatness; that of Europe as a whole, reviving both herself and her claim to a central position in any kind of world, including the ultramodern; and finally, that of the Eastern Europeans, seeking revision of the "final" dispositions of one or another of the two world wars that had begun in their midst.

Such common interests are almost certainly there and may be growing. But, as between the United States and the Soviet Union, some community of political interests may not be sufficient to compensate for inequality in

[2] See *The New York Times,* November 25, 1966, and December 16, 1966, respectively.

most elements of economic power. A sort of condominium in the nuclear field is possible because it can be credibly predicated on the assumption that both of the two superpowers have "won" the arms race; they both have the capacity reciprocally to deter and destroy one another while, in regard to third countries, both stand to lose the fruits of their victory, defined as reciprocal stability and individual security. Anything like a condominium in the economic field is, conversely, necessarily a reflection of the fact that, as of now, the Soviet Union has "lost" its bid to reach production parity; and it might be read to institutionalize the fact that the Soviet Union has come to terms with its defeat as an irreversible one in the foreseeable future. A "sincere" Soviet acceptance of a "sincere" American invitation to participate in the Marshall Plan would have impeded a militant expression of the Soviet bid for parity to the point of standstill before the cold war reached its culminating point. Similarly, a "sincere" agreement by the Soviet Union to be in any meaningful way associated with an organization like the OECD would signify that the Soviets are prepared to make the best of America's politicoeconomic preponderance in Europe and the world at large even before they had seriously attempted to check it with the aid of a policy of detente. For if the original combination of Economic Cooperation Administration–Organization for European Economic Cooperation was a first step toward cushioning the impact on others of the incipient rise of West Germany, the attempt to pull the Soviet Union directly or by way of the lesser Eastern European states into the orbit of American economic power would make sense for the United States mainly as a henceforth feasible shift to an organic containment of the Soviet Union within an OECD type of organization and to the Soviets only as a means of cushioning and up to a point concealing their incipient, but for all practical purposes irreversible, relative decline.

Unless this were tacitly accepted to be the case by all parties, any far-reaching economic co-operation with the Eastern European powers could not but unfold in the context of an ongoing and still undecided growth race with strategic-security implications. As such it would be frustrated in advance in its own terms and have a considerable potential to act as a political irritant. It would arouse suspicions of being exploited for the purpose of enhancing strategic strength by Communists posing as co-operatives or as being managed for the purpose of transforming Communists into consumers first and foremost.

This is not to say that American policy makers will or should not find it attractive to experiment with a once-British formula which cannot but have considerable appeal for a globally extended power situated at some but not altogether safe distance from the shores of Continental Europe. In the early eighteenth and early nineteenth centuries—after the two French bids for hegemony—and again in the late nineteenth century—after Germany's unification but before her global bid—England exchanged her famed policy of a balancer for that of a leaner—on the strongest, but actually or presumably, moderate and conservative Continental power: France, Russia, and Germany, respectively. The factual or formalized alliance entailed for England a release of her full resource for global horizons; for the Continental power it entailed a task and a position. The task was to use local influence and power for controlling or pacifying forces of real or potential disturbance: France to help pacify the Baltic; Russia to uphold the conservative Vienna settlement without making Britain either support or oppose her action in a conspicuous manner; Germany to maintain equilibrium and peace in areas abutting on the Straits —if and as long as willing. The position Britain conceded to the Continental power was that of sufficient pre-eminence on the Continent to enable the Continental ally or associate to carry out his tasks; if any position outside Europe was envisaged, it was one just sufficient to keep the "brilliant second" disposed to back the world empire in critical situations. Consequently, while a sort of Continental ascendancy would be legitimized, the secondary status vis-à-vis the global empire would be confirmed; the inferior partner in an unequal condominium, if such it was or was meant to be, would be kept in line by the world power's retaining its capacity to activate a coalition against the unruly partner and by the ongoing expansion of its over-all position in the world at large.

Historically, the lopsided condominium policy did not fare too well. No great Continental power was prepared for any length of time to enjoy and endure this kind of consecration by the maritime power wielding the trident, just as none had been willing earlier lastingly to submit to the spiritual power wearing the triple crown. Reduced and internally unstable, France cooperated for a time after the Peace of Utrecht. Russia, with Continental and overseas ambitions of her own, could not be kept in line more than intermittently after the Congress of Vienna. Austria failed as the second-best substitute for the ostensibly strongest single continental power. And Germany, while pursuing under Bismarck, for her own good reasons, conservative policies in keeping with over-all British desires, would not have Pomeranian grenadiers die for Constantinople any more than she would later pull England's chestnuts out of the embers of China. Instead, sooner or later—if ultimately always in vain—the foremost Continental state ended up by seeking to forge the unity of the Continent against the empire of the seas—France by way of the Diplomatic Revolution, which imperfectly wrote finis to her secular hostility with the Habsburgs; Russia by means of the Holy Alliance, which can properly be interpreted as in large part a secular policy aimed at directing autocratic Continental states against both parliamentary and maritime England while excluding, along with her, the at-once Moslem and Straits-blocking Ottoman Empire; and Germany by means of the Kaiser's ineffectual pursuit of the myth of the European Combine.

The policy is thus discredited from the perspective of history, but no more than is its alternative, Continental unity; if properly adjusted to contemporary conditions, it may even succeed temporarily. The key factors are the contemporary significance of the normally laggard and imperfect operation of the balance of power between empires and the strength of the imperial states vis-à-vis the over-all system in which they function.

In regard to the balance of power, the great unknown is the real and locally perceived extent of Soviet present weakness relative to the United States. The situation of Soviet Russia after the exertions under Stalin and Khrushchev may be somewhat like that of France, who, when weary in body and soul from the Sun King's policy of magnificence was in addition beset by a junior partner's desire for supreme status within the dynastic family system and for territory at its periphery. If this is so, Soviet Russia, beset by Communist China as Bourbon France was by Bourbon Spain, might be as ready to seek aid and comfort from the United

States in regard to her domestic needs, European dependents, and Asian enemy, as France sought it across the Channel under the guise of a shared concern for pacifying the universe—and, of course, as an alternative to being taken in the vise of pressures from traditional enemies and a recent ally. In so doing, Russia can expect to get fairly good terms from the United States, just as France did from Great Britain. It is not in America's interest to reunify the world Communist movement and the power of the two greatest states of Eurasia under the triumphant sway of a Sinified version of Stalinism, any more than it was in England's to help Philip V achieve that which she had fought both his Habsburg namesake and his Bourbon ancestor to prevent—a direct or indirect unification of the Continental power and overseas possessions of France and Spain.

Conversely, however, the Soviet Union may feel strong enough to do without America's backing or not sufficiently strong to bear such backing, however discreet. In the first instance the Soviet Union might decide to retrench its external activities and withdraw for the purpose of strengthening its material stance behind a nuclear missile shield vis-à-vis the United States, a conventional military wall vis-à-vis China, and the diplomatic screen of an active but reasonable diplomacy vis-à-vis all the world—except for occasional sallies into revolution-like behavior in well-chosen situations for the sake of upholding a tradition and maintaining a claim. In the second instance the Soviets would have to go completely inactive or else seek strenuously for compensatory strength outside the United States rather than accept the position of America's secondary partner in and for a definitely pacified Europe and of her second in the search for peace in Asia. This would be the case especially if the United States were to derive additional economic, military, and diplomatic strength from a successful conclusion of the war in Vietnam.

The more than usually great difficulty in estimating the present and imminent, real and experienced, power means of empires militates against a firm conclusion. So does the difficulty of assessing the extent to which physical vastness, qualified by communications, combines with universality of claims, revitalized by ideology, to act as significant obstacles to the balancing of finite power and objectives. The intangibles of ideology and status, moreover, operate differently and tend to frustrate one another between any two of the three states with imperial role or pretension—the United States, the Soviet Union, and Communist China; while the implications of nuclear weaponry remain unknown when it comes to behavior that has moved beyond the zone where political action can and does proceed in an "as if" manner—as if, that is, in isolation from the ultimate instrument in the *ultima ratio* of realms. In such circumstances analysis and prediction must be informed by the reminder that contemporary empires partake of both the instincts and the institutions of states and that they operate in an international system which, however modified by the presence in it of a pre-eminent power and of at least two imperial states, is not free of the historically evolved and structurally induced expedients, constraints, and sheer frustrations for the strongest of powers implicit in any halfway crystallized such system.

As states, both the United States and the Soviet Union are unlikely to make, out of a sense of ultimately invulnerable substance, the sacrifices in either material safeguards or prestige sensitivities which would make easy or possible a transition from acute conflict to ultimate co-operation. As powers in an international system, they do not possess either the degree of relative freedom or the same shortage of options (both tending to make absolute solutions attractive or even mandatory) enjoyed and endured by historic empires, whatever degree of comparable tendencies or temptations the modern empires may be heir to. The farther one goes back in antiquity, the stronger do individual powers appear in their capacity both to generate new and to constrain established power relative to comparable capacity of the inchoate systems in which they were loosely fitted. Only after the fall of the last ancient, Roman, empire, did the balance between actors and system appear to have shifted and the international system, however primitive itself and weak in both constraining and generative capacity, appear as stronger than the still more primitive and weaker individual realms. More than one shift in relative dominance has since occurred, as the system centered on Europe has evolved toward maturity and decay. At its outset, the contemporary global system was quite strong—if one considers the considerable potential for constraining established power and generating new or strengthened actors which was implicit in the sustained and long-inconclusive conflict between the two major states, which conflict defined the system even if it was not wholly coterminous with it. The system was certainly "stronger" in these terms than it would have been had the two powers been either disposed or able to carry their conflict to military resolution in the relatively short run—considering the relative insignificance of the military power and the facilities of third states sufficiently valuable and hard to get to inflect superpower behavior as part of a wartime contest for control. In consequence, the systemic requirements of a nonwar competition tended to supplement the political intelligence and corrected the historic and ideological idiosyncracies of the in some ways primitive super-power actors—by means not entirely different from those operative during the early medieval European system. Originating in the exclusion of major war, systemic constraints were progressively reinforced by and combined with systemic opportunities; these latter resulted from the reinclusion as relatively independent political actors of additional, first small and subsequently major if still middling, powers.

One result has been of special significance. When contemplating the respective attractions of conquest and, more recently, of withdrawal or condominium, the imperial powers have not faced only one another, or only a third power threatening to both. They have had also to reckon with a growing array of other states with whom they could co-operate in order to avoid the costs of a premature accommodation and had to expect to co-operate again should such accommodation fail. These states have been more or less anxious to discourage any existing propensity to either withdrawal or condominial deal by either or both of the super-powers. In so doing some of them have been harping on the consequences of their political weakness or military vulnerability if kept out of a deal or left to their own devices—for example, West Germany in Europe and, say, Thailand in Asia—while others have been playing up their diplomatic utility (even if not military strength) if fitted into this or that countervailing strategy: for example, the Philippines in regard to the military-political containment of China in Asia and France in regard to the politicoeconomic containment of the United States in Europe. At the same time, activist governments of certain undeveloped countries tried to lead in drafting China to counteract the politi-coeconomic preponderance of both industrial super-powers or at least in contributing toward keeping them apart. Whoever may lead wheresoever, however, no state is likely to stand still while the world order is being stabilized by a Soviet-American agreement or thrown into imbalance by the withdrawal into passivity of one or the other. Nor is any state likely in either—or any—case to avoid seeking new roles in new regional and global balances of power and influence as it watches the devitalization of the roles rooted in the old Soviet-American balance—whether the state be Britain or Poland in Europe, Japan or India in Asia.

The reordering into which each state can fit itself as such a reordering emerges from the ebb and flow of containment and countercontainment on a lowered level of intensity and tension is apt to be the result of specific deeds, not sweeping deals. And world equilibrium is not apt to be comprised in any artifice of simulated balance between unequal superpowers, but rather to be the not quite or always intended resultant of complementary imbalances in individual regions or segments, adding up to an over-all equilibrium under the leadership of the United States as the globally primary power. There is no more (or less) contradiction between leadership and equilibrium in relation to variously strong and unevenly expansionist great states than there is in relation to variously big and dynamic firms in the theory and practice of oligopoly. The principle of complementary imbalances applies to the entire system. It will be sketched out in the following pages with respect to Europe and the less developed segment of the world.

Leadership can assume different forms in different areas. In Europe more than anywhere else American leadership can henceforth best be exercised by way of delegation of initiatives to European powers best suited by their particular position and by the over-all international constellation to promote the achievement of common or generally acceptable goals. The extent to which the United States will or ought to underwrite such initiatives by guaranteeing those undertaking them against the consequences of failure is a key question. The answer to it will depend on the extent to which the European powers will allow themselves to be circumscribed in their initiatives by common caution and by commitment to shared ideals, even if not by too conspicuous complicities and limitations that would annul the diplomatic worth of their initiatives and erode the moral significance of their independence.

Diplomacy in the late 1960s and beyond is apt to be one of fluidity, not so much revolutionary as revolving around European settlement and Afro-Asian unsettlement. The Soviet Union is apt to grope for a new synthesis in its policies toward Europe and Afro-Asia which would reconcile Stalin's concentration on Europe and Khrushchev's fascination with world policy on a lower level of intensity which can be sustained in the long pull. As for the United States, it may be compelled to shift ever more attention and resource to Asia, while groping for an authentic world policy that is free from historically bred emotional attachments to any particular country or continent. The lesser industrialized powers of Western and, within limits, Eastern Europe—as well as Japan in Asia—are apt to waver between the suddenly multiplying options, flirting with some or all in turn without committing themselves fully to any new course, anxious to be friends with everyone and antagonize no one definitively. In that respect at least they may end up practicing the basic strategies of the unaligned countries in the 1950s and incur with more style but less excuse the limited risks and total frustrations of agitated futility. The "new" diplomacy tends to be one without either substantial prizes or severe penalties in an international system with few lasting consummations. These may be the exactly right external counterparts to the internal processes of mature industrial societies, permissive with respect to everything but major violence and overpowering aggregations. Alternatively, of course, insubstantial multistate diplomacy may follow into discredit its cold war predecessor, the multilateral parliamentary diplomacy of the United Nations. It might then give way to stabler, more predictable, and even authoritative modes of ordering international life, just as the futilities of the parliamentary system have given way to more settled modes within some industrialized countries characterized by diminishing civil strife but continuing excess of political over civic spirit. With regard to Western Europe, the so far frustrating pattern of staggered turnover in personnel and foreign policies may yet reverse itself into a favorable conjunction of personalities and pressures inclined and inclining toward a more stable association. To be significant in the larger picture, a Western European association would have to be sufficiently strong to counterpoise the eastern half of the Continent and sufficiently independent to cooperate with it for European unity and global equilibrium—a unity which, we have noted earlier, may in the end come to depend on the institutionally more primitive East if single-minded commitment is to do the work of singlehanded conquest. A workable policy for Western Europe must eventually fuse into one the two temporal phases of de Gaulle's European policy: to approach the Soviet Union on the basis of common strength (which meant, in the early 1960s, Franco-German strength to be based on an implemented Treaty of Friendship) as well as on the basis of common interests (meaning, in the mid-1960s, Franco-Soviet interests, in regard to Germany and the United States). These two approaches may have been reciprocally exclusive in terms of strictly national and Continental diplomacy; the extent to which this was so may be lessened, with luck and skill, in the framework of a concerted all-European policy with global implications, supplying a greater scope for controlling the elements of heterogenity and inequalities in the domain of "common strength" and for orchestrating the elements of harmony in the realm of "common interests."

In the meantime, while it is being decided whether the preconditions of more substantial achievements can take shape in the terms of both objective structures and subjective orientations, it may be of some use to work out variations on tactical approaches on the one hand and schematic models of the best of all possible worlds on the other.[1] The former concerns the so-called policy of peaceful engagement, aimed at isolating East Germany by reassuring everyone else in Eastern Europe by trade and pledges (chiefly directed at West Germany); the latter deals with carefully contrived balances of military power-cum-arms controls between a Western Europe integrated under U.S. auspices on the one hand and the Soviet Union on the other. The first approach is a substitute for policy for the late 1960s highly attractive to policy makers pressed to revise old policies without having new ones; the second approach was a possibility in the late 1950s and continues to be attractive to schematic speculators immune to intervening changes in the world scene.

[1] The following passages through the paragraph on p. 72 ending with the words "pure and simple" is a word for word reproduction of a memorandum that the author made available just before General de Gaulle's visit in the Soviet Union in the summer of 1966 to the Foreign Relations Committee of the U.S. Senate, as a background paper for the Committee's hearings on U.S. policies toward Europe. The policy of peaceful engagement was formulated in the greatest detail in Zbigniew Brzezinski's *Alternative to Partition* (New York: 1965). The term "peaceful engagement" is now used in two places instead of the "peaceful re-engagement" in the original document.

For the West to contrive anything like a quantitative equipoise of indigenous military forces on the European continent would be tantamount to a Soviet defeat of the first magnitude as long as the Russians are weakened by China in their rear and the West Europeans continue to be reinforced by the United States in theirs. Soviet influence in Eastern Europe would be definitively jeopardized, compelling Soviet leaders to consider desperate resorts internally and externally as an alternative to facing a situation on their Western frontier which would provide Germany with a third chance for conquest, this time apt to be successful because ostensibly peaceful and morally underwritten by the West, at least initially.

The more promising and in the long run more likely world equilibrium is (to repeat) a different one. It consists of the Soviet Union occupying the position of the foremost European power, parallelling and in part offsetting America's primacy in the world system at large. The existence of a first or foremost power, capable in principle and temporarily in practice to inflict military defeat on the rest of the European states, has been a recurrent feature of European politics. It is compatible with such a power being diplomatically hemmed in most of the time with the aid of the complexity of interests and impossibility constantly to threaten force even in prenuclear conditions; and it is compatible with such power being militarily checked with the aid of an extra-European power whenever it sets out to transform political primacy into military hegemony. The United States is currently in Britain's position with regard to a Europe where Soviet Russia is assuming the place of pre-Napoleonic France and pre-Wilhelminian Germany. A world system of complementary imbalances (favoring the Soviet Union in Europe and the United States globally) is admittedly imperfect but also the most likely one to work. New conditions, including nuclear deterrence and economic prosperity in industrialized countries, are strong material safeguards against the system re-enacting the hitherto periodic breakdowns in a major war. Arms-control devices could only marginally add to the more fundamental restraints. The salient task for Western diplomacy, also in view of the rise of Communist China, is to bring Soviet leadership face to face with a politically meaningful choice between the ideological goal of world dominion and the traditional goal of Russia as the last European power in line of succession to a widely acknowledged, because on balance and most of the time beneficial, political primacy in Europe. The choice can be rendered practically meaningful only by the certain prospect of the United States progressively reducing its pervasive political and economic involvement in Western Europe as the new ordering in Europe takes shape, without abandoning its ultimate military security guarantee. Such a reduction of involvement can be deliberate and risk being precipitate; or, preferably, it can take the form of a statesmanlike acceptance of the progressive extrusion of American presence as alternatives to it materialize. The opposite policy is that of fostering divisions among Europeans as a means to perpetuating such presence. In the absence of such divisive American strategy, it would be self-defeating folly for the Soviet Union to try to exploit any increase of differences among individual Western European states that would attend their emancipation from invisible American tutelage and conspicuously visible American protection. Such exploitative strategy would be the surest way to drive the West Europeans back into the American fold, thus undoing the chief gain the Soviets could hope to derive from the shift of the over-all global balance of power to their disadvantage—a shift which is, of course, the precondition of their political acceptability in Europe for Europeans.

The initial cost of the new European arrangement will be borne by Germany, just as it was borne by France when she was struck down from the heights of expansionist power. It is in the interest of the Germans to accept, without raising the automatic cry of discrimination, an elementary fact, to wit, that they must work their way back into the international system on each and every level as the system moves toward something like normalcy. They started from scratch and moved up, patiently enough at first, in the West European and the Atlantic frameworks; they must be prepared to go down a bit before they can hope to move forward and upward again in a reconstructed all-European and global framework. The extent to which they accept the inevitable, including some diminution of previously acquired status in exchange for some increase in prospects for attainment of substantive political goals (bearing on the attenuation of divisions between West and East Germany), will determine the thrust and the degree of Franco-Russian co-operation in regard to Central Europe. It is not in the long-term interest of the United States to overburden this aspect by countenancing German sensibilities.

Like so often before, Great Britain can be expected to rally to the new political trend once it appears to be irreversible, if only in the hope of preventing the trend from working lastingly against her. To associate a British government as presently disposed with a European diplomatic reconstruction from the beginning would introduce into the process from the Western side all the half-heartedness about ends and ambiguity about motives which would doom it from the start and render the strategy suspect in Soviet eyes. The take-off of a European strategy for Europe depends now on France and Soviet Russia; only in the subsequent phase will the momentum and outcome of something like self-sustaining political development in Europe depend on a satisfactory insertion of Great Britain and on a satisfactory definition by the West Germans of their irreducible but also final national goals. The reason for this two-phase progression is this: only as a preliminary Franco-Russian entente, over procedure at the very least, demonstrates that practical complements or alternatives to the military-political Atlantic framework do exist, and that they can create new opportunities without forfeit of essential security, will the necessary internal pressure be generated to inflect governmental policies in Germany and, less dramatically but no less essentially, in Great Britain toward a new course.[2]

In a reordered European system, Eastern Europe would continue to evolve under lessened but legitimized Soviet paramountcy, exercised in more or less explicit agreement between the Soviet Union and France (and eventually Great Britain) over its terms and limits. The continuation of such paramountcy will be ac-

---

[2] This evolution has begun to take place since these lines were written and has manifested itself in Britain's renewed interest in joining the Common Market and in Soviet Premier Kosygin's demonstrations of European spirit and Soviet-British friendship in London in February, 1967. The Soviet attempt to take advantage of the newly displayed "Gaullist" streak in Prime Minister Wilson's European policy is doubtless intended to encourage the British to move somewhat further away from the American connection; it may also be intended to encourage General de Gaulle to move yet closer to Soviet theses, on East Germany and a European security pact, so as to keep one step ahead in the detente sweepstakes.

cepted even (or, paradoxically, especially) by non-Communists on strictly pragmatic grounds as the necessary safeguard against two foremost and complementary dangers for key countries in the area—an excessive interest in it by Germany and the lack of reliably persistent interest in it, for its own sake, on the part of the foremost Western power of the moment: France before she desperately needed allies against a stronger Germany, Britain in the interwar period, and the United States whenever relations with the Soviet Union permit. Insofar as Western European economic performance can be kept up without premature consolidation of political institutions (especially those of a liberal-parliamentary character) and the Soviet Union can be shown that it cannot hold Eastern Europe indefinitely without somebody's co-operation in the West—a co-operation to be had for a price that would not be subject to arbitrary increase with every failing of Soviet power—the present evolution in Eastern Europe can be expected to continue without the risk of forcible reversal from without or the probability of indefinite reversibility from within.

The power appointed by geography and history to be the partner of the Soviet Union at this time and for some time to come is France, because rather than despite the fact that she is much weaker than the United States in material power and even in sentimental attractiveness for most Eastern Europeans. This fact is not due to anything so transient and accidental as the current American military involvement in Asia. And it is not likely to be undone by a common American-Soviet front against Red China once the Vietnamese conflict is over; the two superpowers will continue to hope for different things and fear different things in regard to China for long enough to delay past the potentially fruitful moment the practical expression of an ultimate solidarity against the newcomer.

The key impediment to a U.S.–U.S.S.R. settlement of European questions rests rather in the basic incompatibility of American and Soviet interest as far as Europe is concerned. The Soviets cannot but hold back from co-operating in a European reconstruction through procedures and for ends agreeable to the United States. To act otherwise after the failure of their own forward thrust in the Caribbean and without prospect for compensation by way of access to new geopolitical areas of influence would be to formalize Soviet Russia's inferior standing in superpower relations. In exchange they can expect nothing more tangible than continued American self-restraint with regard to the question of nuclear weapons for Germany and self-interested American co-operation in slowing down or inhibiting nuclear proliferation in general. Both of these pay-offs are, however, likely to recede in importance as alternative forms for containing Germany take shape and as nuclear proliferation in countries other than Germany bogs down or else progresses without catastrophic results for Soviet security and the international system. The United States is not in a substantially better position. It is likely to find it impossible to reinterpret America's moral and political commitments in Europe, and not least to the West German regime, in such a way as to secure enough leeway for a practical compromise with the Soviet Union. Such compromise would largely have to meet Soviet ideas for European security and political order in form, while guaranteeing the West against forcible or other reversals in existing trends and conditions which have been depriving these forms of much of their expansionist potential. While the American military-political commitments continue in their irreducible ultimate sense, a continental European power like France can more conveniently proceed in this direction than the U.S., which can hardly maintain existing commitments and explore creative political alternatives to them without seeing the fabric of American policies in Western Europe disintegrate before a new one is spun complete.[3]

It is in these conditions that reside the ultimate complementarity of French and American assets (and within reason, informed by awareness of the complementarity, of French and American strategies) and the futility of an American attempt to steal de Gaulle's thunder by outdoing him with competitive approaches to Eastern Europeans. Such an attempt might wreck the French strategy (although even this is not certain) by making the Eastern Europeans meet factics with tactics and hold out for ever better terms without fear of seeing the West's disposition to a detente wither away; but the attempt cannot supplant the French strategy with a more effective, or safer, variety.

The essence of the political crisis as it concerns Europe is this: A constellation exists in Europe and in the world at large when the Soviet Union can be brought face to face with a fair choice between policies, one of which can satisfy its legitimate interests as a major power in a way which would be compatible with the West's basic World War II goals, without unduly endangering the West militarily in view of the concurrent change in political climate. The Soviet

---

[3] This argument has been somewhat weakened by the intervening changes in West German government and policies in December, 1966, and the resulting outward changes in the over-all NATO political orientation. See *The New York Times,* Dec. 17, 1966, p. 13, for commentary.

Union may be unready for such a course, because of lingering ideological and power commitments to larger goals; because it will finally shrink back from remaking frozen patterns as much as the United States seems to; or because the Soviets might fear that a policy of detente centered on European powers rather than on the United States would bring upon them the political retaliation of the United States, which would directly or indirectly feed into the pressures coming from Red China. The foreign policy of the United States can foster or impede this vital exploration of basic Soviet intentions at this point, with different risks and rewards in each case. But it cannot spirit away the fact that such exploration is the necessary preliminary to any new long-term reordering of relationships in the West, just as the dislocation by de Gaulle of the postwar alliance pattern was the necessary preliminary to the meaningfulness of the "opening to the East"—whatever else may be argued by proponents of peaceful engagement pure and simple.

The situation is one rich in paradoxes as well as problems. The United States can best exert leadership vis-à-vis the Western European powers if it tacitly delegates most initiatives; it can secure a maximum of the substance of co-operation with the Soviet Union in Europe at large if it accepts a measure of Soviet competition against the United States in co-operation with the Western European powers; and the United States will fare best in regard to Eastern Europe if it establishes a clear and conspicuous distinction between the margin of politicoeconomic access to that region which is apparently possible and that which it actually utilizes, the difference being useful for deterrence of and bargaining over Soviet initiatives elsewhere. Ambiguity of co-operative–competitive relations between the United

States and the Soviet Union across the entire spectrum is more likely than is any neat division between co-operation in Europe and competition in the extra-European world, or vice versa. Staying somewhat aloof from Eastern Europe will permit American policy to assign Eastern Europe a place in its global strategy which it can uphold indefinitely, regardless of passing fads and enthusiasms, while minimizing the capacity of the Eastern European regimes to make the Western powers compete over the status of the politically "most favored nation" in Eastern Europe. The danger of such a competition is a more imminent and serious problem than that of the Soviet Union exploiting divisions among Western Europeans or between Western Europeans and the United States for deals with some and dominance over all. As for West Germany, she can best secure meaningful political pay-offs for her economic efforts in Eastern Europe if she lets France collect them for her—against commission; and she can best reassure East Europeans as to her future objectives not only or chiefly by solemn renunciations for the future but by a present readiness and action. The crux is German co-operation toward bringing about constellations among the great powers, including the United States, which would at once circumscribe the capacity of any future German government to exploit, and the disposition of any other great power to permit, a revival of revisionist tendencies and resulting instabilities in Eastern Europe which might provide an opening as well as a precedent for German revisionism —a revisionism, it is worth noting, which is least threatening to the Southeastern European countries, which have active territorial claims of their own.

A constellation constraining Germany and reassuring to the East Europeans with reason to fear her cannot be evolved within a purely Western European setting, unless the United States stays in indefinitely as a full-time regional policeman. German consent to configurational constraints cannot in turn be secured for any length of time without some major achievement toward however loose and heterogeneous a unification. Moreover, it would be difficult to maintain any kind of constraint over even a loosely reunited Germany during a sufficiently long probation period, unless both Germany and the United States accept the fact and the implications of the survival, in a "new" or "greater" Europe, of a Franco-Soviet "special relationship"; such a relationship, possibly extended somehow to encompass Great Britain, is apt to be necessary if only for the purpose of one specific, Continental, and if necessary military, containment (of Germany) and one general, all-European or global, and only politico-economic, counterpoise (vis-à-vis the United States). Despite the vast disparity in military strength between France and Russia, the Soviets may well conclude that they need France to keep Western Europe quiet and any American action awkward or illegitimate, should good reasons arise for intervening militarily against a resurgent Germany about to go nuclear. They can begin to think about easing the Soviet position on German "unification" only when they are certain of the political premises of such a constellation; similarly, the French can contemplate rendering the just-mentioned political service to Russia and Europe only if a minimum nuclear deterrent power protects them against a misjudgment of the motives (or, should worst come to worst, against an error in the estimate of Soviet intentions) of a French government prepared morally to guarantee the limited object of a Soviet Russia acting as Europe's mandatory within the confines of Germany.

The best available institutional expression of the new configuration may prove to be a species of a European security pact, built around the Soviet Union as Europe's foremost power, implicitly aimed at West Germany as Europe's physical center and psychological point of common concern, and circumscribed in the last resort by the strategic vigilance of the United States as the condition of Western Europe's self-confidence vis-à-vis Soviet Russia. Politically in part disengaged from Europe—following the attainment of the principal goals of its post-World War II diplomacy —the United States would be liberated for an even-handed world policy. Politically reinforced in Europe, by an institutionalized admission of their European role, the Soviets might feel able to lead Eastern Europe into economic co-operation with the West, rather than using established economic ties with the Eastern Europeans and the emerging economic and political ties with the Western Europeans to impede or disrupt links with the United States. A Soviet-sponsored European security pact may prove to be the necessary, if not necessarily sufficient or easy to mesh, complement of an American-inspired OECD extended eastward. West Germany, in turn, may accept to co-operate with her own containment—by accepting the implicit thrust of the European security pact and her initially secondary position in it—in the legitimate hope that the new framework would prove more productive of acceptable political and institutional ties with East Germany and of a both profitable and prestigious politicoeconomic role in Central-Eastern Europe than any alternative framework. Bonn might be all the more co-operative should it become progressively apparent that its only alternative was neither a preferentially intimate alliance with the United States nor a specially close com-

munity with France, but a posture of diplomatic isolation—since, if West Germany previously felt unable to
choose between the United States and France, neither
France nor the United States is likely to rush into a
choice between West Germany and Soviet Russia favorable to the Germans in the future. A posture of
diplomatic isolation, however, would deprive West
Germany of any stable role and might force her eventually to bid for regional primacy in Central-Eastern
Europe from a vulnerable security position on the
strength of economic "co-operation" and, possibly, nuclear "independence." The hoped-for prospect of such
strategy might be that of peacefully colonizing East
Germany and Central-Eastern Europe, if only economically on the face of it; the dismal possibility would
be for West Germany to be recolonized politically as
a consequence of a Soviet military intervention implementing the mandate of a Europe which would thus be
made against, rather than with, Germany.

As for the Europe between Germany and Russia, the
first thing to realize is that policies that were too difficult to manage with regard to Western Europe are
unlikely to be more manageable in regard to Eastern
Europe—both generally and for the United States in
particular. One problem is to decide whether to direct
Western policy primarily to governments or to peoples.
This may mean, for instance, whether to recognize or
have the Germans recognize the Oder-Neisse frontier
line as a means for promoting reconciliation between
Poles and Germans or also (or primarily) as a means
of embarrassing the Polish Communist government
(insofar as it derives internal support or toleration
from widespread insecurity feelings vis-à-vis Germany
and her allies). The United States has a special reason
to appreciate the difference, since it did not fare so

well with its contradictory policy of supporting reconciliation between the French and the Germans while inhibiting exclusive governmental intimacies on the level of high policy.

The difference between the governmental and the popular levels is vital for both the Western and the Eastern European powers, however much it may be slurred over by notions of a gradual liberalization process. The ideal for the Eastern European regimes is to reduce the Soviet say in their domestic and foreign policies without forfeiting the needed measure of Soviet support for control over their own peoples. In the Polish case, this may mean specifically the reduction of Soviet involvement in East Germany as long as Moscow's concert with Paris matches the efficacy of its present controls in Pankow, and Warsaw gains from the change in the nature of its "central" position. More generally, all or most Eastern European regimes may well feel that an intra-European East-West concert is better suited to realize their twin objective than an intense involvement by the United States would be. They may well calculate that in cases of domestic upheavals against regimes weakened internally or externally (by the intensification of political currents and reduction of Soviet supports attendant on "bridge-building"), a susceptibility of American policy makers to overreaction at any time and a receptivity to ethnic minority pressures at election time might result in support for drastic internal changes should the danger of a major conflagration appear less than in the 1950s. Conversely, the Communist regimes may regard the Western European governments as more reliably interested in preserving a balanced situation in Europe as a condition of their own security and diplomatic independence—the "balanced situation" entailing Soviet preponderance in Eastern Europe as a whole and, as its price and premise, Communist party preponderance within the Eastern European countries individually. Hence the Western European governments can be counted upon to discountenance bids for radical or sudden change in Eastern Europe as liable to produce either Soviet reassertion, and thus undermine the European settlement based on detente and consequent reduction of American presence, or Soviet frustration, leading to a withdrawal of Soviet power from Eastern Europe and leaving Western Europe without a graduated Soviet counterpoise to Germany in situations short of major war.

If these or comparable considerations do gain currency in Eastern Europe, then the Western Europeans might be partners not only preferred to Americans but also better able to secure practicable political returns on the West's contribution to the economic strength and political legitimation of Communist regimes. A return commensurate with the Western outlay is one that complements external with internal political diversification while stabilizing to the greatest possible extent both the new outside links and the inner transformations which are implicit in the process of transition from a Soviet-bloc to a European-association policy. Such diversification and stabilization are not likely to be feasible by means of basic constitutional revisions entailing elections that would reintroduce reconstructed political parties into revitalized parliaments. They can be promoted with more effect by way of a freer access to top-level executive positions; in the domain of foreign political and economic policy making they can best be achieved by individuals with independent views and authority to assert them, regardless of their past affiliations. The immediate objective of Western policy ought therefore to be not so much the juridical revival of, say, the peasant or shopkeeper parties as the *de facto* reformation of English, French, American, etc., "parties" among high officials prepared and able to argue with the Soviet "party" the advantages of specific commitments and rapprochements from broadly shared fundamental premises. The presence of conspicuously independent-minded officials in the inner councils of state would be the nearest substitute for the vitalizing effect of free public opinion in the Communist countries themselves. For the West, such internal changes would represent the nearest thing to a guarantee of the seriousness of an East European regime ostensibly prepared to move in a new direction externally—just as the removal of such men from their position of influence would indicate yet another change of course.

American policy toward Western Europe failed when attempting an implicit barter between American economic assistance and basic institutional transformations in Western Europe. In the end, the issue of Western European future in unity or disunity came to turn on the interplay between more or less compelling material forces and more or less strong-willed personalities. Both the United States and the Western European powers would overreach themselves if they tried to do more than stimulate such an interplay in an Eastern Europe that only begins to be accessible to either stick or carrot, pressure or inducement. By the same token, one cannot expect miracles in regard to Eastern Europe from institutions of multilateral cooperation, which although they did some good failed to be the *summum bonum* for Western Europe. Neither, however, ought the Western governments to make a free gift of their readiness to aid and legitimize regimes interposed between themselves and still virtually voiceless peoples, in their own interests. However decisive the subterraneous sociopolitical processes in matters like these may be in the end, diplomacy deals and can only deal on a highly personal level with the visible symptoms and symbols of such processes, while statecraft must seek to encompass both—process and symptom, symbols as well as interests and power.

II.

ALLIANCES AND INTERVENTION: AMERICA FACING HER HEMISPHERE AND AFRO-ASIA

For the United States largely to delegate leadership in Europe and exercise it much more directly in the non-European world would be a matter not of inconsistency but of conditions. The basic structural features in the matter are two. First there is the presence or absence in either area of local powers capable of constituting something like material weights in, and displaying political intelligence or readiness for, a contemporary facsimile of the balance of power. Europe has these basic indigenous ingredients and requires therefore extraregional elements of only a special kind in carefully rationed quantities; neither Asia nor Africa nor Latin America have (or believe they need) them —yet. The second factor concerns the identity of the regional candidate for primacy or paramountcy—that is, his capacity for being moderated by admission to a role of responsibility by other members of the area. The cardinal assumption of this essay—which is open to contradiction by argument and refutation by events —has been that Europe is beginning to have such power now in Soviet Russia, or at least that she will not know whether she does or does not until the European powers have agreed among themselves to act on that assumption as a means of testing it. The contrary assumption has been that Asia does not have in China a respectable power capable of exercising wider responsibilities and that neither Latin America nor Africa has so far produced an indigenous regional power even remotely capable of doing more than fend for itself on a day-by-day basis.

In an increasingly pluralistic world encompassing the two major segments of industrially developed and undeveloped countries, the problems for the United States as the primary global power are external and internal. Externally, the basic requirement is to apportion instrumentalities of American control or influence in such ways as to conform to the *genius loci,* interpreted by a local leader of genius or not.

In regard to Europe, the apportionment problem has been shifting from the military to the economic aspect of American power and, consequently, from its public to its private sector. The most conspicuous issue of the day—sharing of control over nuclear weaponry through access to hardware or merely to the committee table—is apt to be supplemented and even superseded by the question of possession and control of the basic theoretical know-how and industrial technology which underlie nuclear military power and are fostered by it in the first place. The issue has assumed the shape of a growing concern over the increasing size of direct American investments in Western Europe in general and the virtually monopolistic position of American-controlled enterprise in the critical or commanding sectors of an ultramodern economy in particular. The concern over economic domination is felt or voiced with unequal strength by governments with different priorities and propagandistic needs; but it is likely to gather strength as it overshadows or merges with the secondary issue of economic or financial hardship resulting from obligatory purchases of American arms as a contribution to common defense.

A growing qualitative as well as quantitative imbalance in industrial power may be less difficult to bear for European governments in the short run than even a diminishing imbalance of international payments has been for an American administration with enough difficulties elsewhere. But now, before the issue becomes a genuinely popular one in Europe and the present governmental equation is upset, may still be the time to disinter old recipes for governmental control of private "dollar imperialism" by counsel and suasion—regardless of whether a reduction of the dollar outflow for private direct investments will or can contribute simultaneously to the reduction of the imbalance of payments. From the viewpoint of American corporations, especially those occupying the politically sensitive because technologically crucial sectors, the choice may be progressively reduced to one of preference for the dangers of eventual dispossession, however indirect or disguised, and immediate moderation. From the viewpoint of politically self-conscious European governments, the choice would seem to concern the ways best suited to dramatize the need for national or joint European alternatives to American capital and know-how and, secondarily, ways most likely to reduce dependence in due course without embittering political relations with the United States. This may or may not revolve around the alternative of either keeping American producers out of Europe and depending on imports from the United States in the short run, or else of encouraging or tolerating physical transplantation of American productive capacity to Europe and relying on some form of meaningful "Europeanization" or intra-European "capitalization" of critical American-controlled enterprises in the long run.

By contrast with Europe, the critical instruments of influence and control to be apportioned in Asia, Africa, and even Latin America—more or less conspicuously and immediately—are still military. If problems of economic investments matter in those areas (just as military matters do in Europe), those of governmental economic aid matter more, and those of American military involvement in crises matter most—if only because economic instruments, however skillfully fitted into strategies of political development, are in themselves incapable of generating either a stable new order based on local responsibility or a sensible new attitude of responsiveness and reciprocity of recipients toward the chief donor. However attractive the opposite view may be for some, there has been no over-all trend in the less developed segment toward greater importance of the economic factor and instrument as compared with the military one. For a long time to come the less developed countries can enjoy no more than short-term fluctuation in emphasis on one or the other factor in the spectrum of political, economic, and military factors and instruments, as ever more diversified (if intermittent) disturbers and disturbances of peace and order succeed one another. An American foreign and military policy professing commitment to the apparently more sophisticated contrary assumption of a perceptible trend from "militarism" to however politicized an "economism" could garner no more than highly precarious political, and very short-term propagandistic, gains. Another contrast with Europe is, moreover, that apportionment in the sense of *dosage* of military intervention does not necessarily connote a sweeping presumption in favor of self-limitation or even abstinence, but merely a bias in favor of selectivity and scale.

The critical domestic requirement varies correspondingly. In regard to Europe, it is to alert a distinct group of Americans to the need of correcting the im-

mediate profit motives by concern for long-range public ends, internationally as well as domestically. In
regard to the less developed areas, it is to blunt the
bitterness and enhance the intellectual significance of
the more or less academic debate engaging members
of all groups of Americans over the utility and legitimacy of American military interventions abroad, to
match the broad consensus reached about the utility
and limitations of economic assistance. One step in this
direction is to segregate the issue of ideological (anti-
Communist) motive from that of long-range policy—
that of promoting gradual transformations toward
largely autonomous regional orders in conditions of
practicable independence even for lesser states and of
blocking contrary approaches. Another step is to realize that not all of the "good things"—such as fixity of
commitments of some anti-Communist governments
and scarcity of nonideological local conflicts—can be
kept from the postwar configuration of rigid bipolarity
and incipient decolonization while getting rid of the
"bad things"—such as excessive anxiety and consequent
contention over minute shifts in allegiance or disposition everywhere and overcommitment to any and every
regime apparently disposed to adopt the superpowers'
view of the dominant conflict.

America's choices and performance in the contemporary international system will be conditioned by several features. The less crucial becomes the fact of
bipolarity—not least because of the unifocal aspect due
to the preponderance of the United States—the more
important becomes long-term coexistence of the more
developed and the less developed segments of what is
also a bisegmental system. The problem of such coexistence, while not historically unprecedented (witness
the interaction of the Greek and Italian city-states with

less developed, if more powerful, states), has genuinely novel dimensions; it is likely to become the critical
issue of world order even if the racial aspect is muted
or neutralized completely. The problem is not necessarily lessened because nonalignment and, especially, its
militant neutralist expression have been fading as a
self-sufficient policy stance with a potential for institutional consolidation. Nonalignment has been eroded by
the tendency of some nonaligned countries (notably
India, which abuts on China) to "more" alignment and
of previously allied countries (notably those abutting
on Soviet Russia, such as Pakistan and Iran) to "less"
alignment. The once-famed doctrine temporarily modifying bipolarism with tripartism in policy (among the
three "worlds," Western, Eastern, and ex-colonial)
receded once bipolarity took a turn toward tripolarity
with the apparent rise of China, and the two superpowers rid bipolarity of its potential for exploitation
by outgrowing their early primitiveness in policy (with
regard to new states, owing to their lack of colonial
experience) and military technology, which made them,
and especially the United States, overrate the strategic
utility as well as political feasibility of permanent
bases. The dissolution of the nonaligned camp has thus
paralleled the disintegration of the two competing
blocs, but with less obviously positive implications for
a new world order. Individual less developed countries
have now been cast adrift on the more than ever un-
charted waters of international relations, and the same
countries collectively, deprived of the comfort of a
protean general doctrine, face the need for choices between alternative specific orientations—toward the new
politics of regional integration or unity; toward traditional patterns of territorial and other conflicts as
part of crystallizing regional subsystems and balances

of power; or toward differentiation and conflict along racial lines, with or without the instigation of a major nonwhite power. Such policy alternatives can be intertwined in practice, but as underlying types of policy they present likewise difficult choices for industrialized major powers and thus for the United States.

Whatever may be the particulars of the coming international system, however, the United States will enjoy an even greater margin for error than it thought to have or acted as if having in the two preceding decades. Both superpowers will be seconded henceforth by inferior but relatively major middle powers which, while largely sharing the ultimate objectives of the ideologically closer of the superpowers, are anxious to supplant them to a degree and exploit their mistakes and handicaps in particular situations, with the result that the middle powers will assume some of the burdens and (even if they do not frustrate one another) facilitate some of the tasks of the superpowers. Moreover, whatever else may be said of the less developed countries, they proved capable of keeping their formal independence or, otherwise put, proved incapable of responding in a conclusive or definitive way to any outside impetus, be it economic aid or political subversion and intervention. The greater margin for error—and for correction of error, contrived by remedial action or automatic by way of compensatory shifts in a field of multiple reacting forces—is apt to apply also to American relations with Communist China. In this relation the Soviet Union will constitute the principal third power until such time as Japan (and India?) gingerly but inescapably feels her way into the harsher inner zone of Asian power politics.

Accordingly, greater political leeway will complement growing military-technological mobility and bring about a real qualitative change. The relevant picture is complete if one adds uncertainty to leeway and mobility. The main features of uncertainty are two: ambivalence of lesser countries toward great-power involvement in their affairs ("Keep great powers out in such a way as to have them back in to a controllable extent when necessary") and doubts as to which local or regional powers in what configurations will eventually fill the conflict vacuum created by the regression of the American-Soviet confrontation. Despite its power and responsibility, the United States is not and will not be capable of determining precisely many local or regional developments, including those of a structural kind. Consequently, American leadership ought to be concerned with manifest threats to international order rather than with hypothetical risks implicit in any reordering of interstate relations. This type of ultimate leadership does not rule out deliberate or consented retraction of controlling influence whenever other, local powers are prepared to take initiatives that the United States is unable to take at all or with comparable effect, if only because each reordering that it supports will be suspected of further increasing its already vaguely disquieting primacy.

But only as regions outside Europe develop the desire and the capacity for establishing a more "normal" and "permanent" order than the existing one will the United States be able to reduce the exercise of global primacy to a common denominator. The denominator would at best consist of a variable compound of cooperation and competition with yet hard-to-identify major new powers and with old, ex-imperial powers such as Great Britain, France, and Japan on the one hand, and of conflict and tacit-or-explicit co-operation with the Communist powers on the other hand. This will probably mean in the first place the Soviet Union; but a shift toward some "tacit" co-operation with Communist China, under the color of reducing the latter's "isolation"—if only as a handy way of retaliating by commensurate means for Soviet Russia's desertion of "superpower solidarity" for "European solidarity"—cannot be ruled out in the aftermath of a setback for the Maoist hard-liners in Peking, whatever may be the initial self-protective verbal radicalism of the "moderates."

Such a mix of competitive–co-operative relations among greater powers is grist to the mill of a great power concert which can be no less effective for being informal and *ad hoc*. A great power concert has also proved compatible in the past with a mutually tolerable distribution of special but not exclusive regional responsibilities for individual major powers; it was even on occasion fostered by such distribution. These responsibilities might well come to be exercised within or by way of regional councils and organizations encompassing small states. The Organization of American States and even more so the Organization of African Unity and the Asian and Pacific Council replicate the Council of Europe rather than the Concert of Europe; they are elements of progress toward realizing, albeit in the loose framework of a world organization, the forms and some of the objectives envisaged prematurely by wartime proponents (including Churchill) of a regionally structured world order. In such a concert system of dovetailing parts, the United States will be all the better able to conduct if it stops insisting on tuning up and playing most or all of the instruments most or all of the time. A measure of detachment from critical local issues was traditionally one of the preconditions of concert leadership, be it that of

Castlereagh's England or Bismarck's Germany. The other precondition is a manifest, but inobtrusive, capacity to bring superior power to bear on the balance of power between other, more directly concerned, states.

In this connection the United States can usefully begin to ask itself some pressing questions. One is whether this country could actually live with the implications of being an *ad hoc* concert leader, should the preconditions of such a concert continue developing. Willingness is not demonstrated by professions of distaste for the role of a global policeman; and the capacity is in doubt not least because of the limited experience and apparently limited temperamental qualification of Americans when it comes to a complex co-operative–competitive interaction with qualitatively comparable major powers—a very different thing from military-political conflict with powerful adversaries and co-operation with subordinate allies. The other question is whether the United States can or will ever accept with good grace the qualitative, even if not quantitative, equalization of the major powers in the area of nuclear capabilities. It can be argued that a purposefully managed selective nuclear proliferation among major industrial or rapidly industrializing powers is thoroughly consistent with a world order managed by several major powers and one primary power.[1] It may even enhance the prospects of order by undercutting the more clearly and immediately disturbing phenomenon of great power instigation or backing for so-called revolutionary wars of liberation in intermediate areas of ethnic, ideological, or constitutional fragmentation. Detention of major nuclear

[1] See Alden Williams (ed.), *op. cit.*

capability is apt to increase the dangers of confrontation with extra- or intraregional nuclear powers; and it is apt to enhance the prospects and comforts of substantial even if not exclusive regional primacy for the regionally strongest power without burdening it with the military risks implicit in gaining, and the political frustrations inseparable from administering, a belt of demanding and undependable, too revolutionary or too reactionary, satellites.

Pending a gradual reordering, which would reduce the extent of American imperial responsibilities in Afro-Asia, but also as a means of promoting such reordering, the United States will be able to draw on a range of instruments. It will continue to practice the relatively new statecraft of economic aid but will not be able to neglect the instruments of traditional statecraft, military-political alliances and military intervention, duly adapted to contemporary desires for emancipation and to realities of continued dependence on the part of lesser, and notably the less developed, states.

Alliances have traditionally been the institutional link between the politics of the balance of power and the politics of preponderance or empire, depending on whether the stress is on aggregating and containing power or on controlling either power or the by-products of its insufficiency. In present conditions the term "alliance" can be employed loosely for mere alignments and vague associations, because even these constitute a serious commitment as long as the ideology of neutralism survives nonalignment as a vital institution and because informal alignments are sufficient between highly unequal powers with little mutuality in performance whenever they enhance the prospect of using superior power with anticipatable effect.

There is quite a range of alternatives with regard to alliances and alignments encompassing less developed countries.[2] An alliance may be primarily aggregative, that is, be designed to add the material or nonmaterial resources of the lesser state or states to American power; preclude the lesser country's alliance with a rival major power; or divert a rival power from damaging initiatives elsewhere by creating a local problem for that power or its small-state ally. To influence the advance toward regional primacy by a local greater power or powers it may suffice to shield the timely creation of the diverse requisites of substantial, if nonprovocative, independence. Or the alliance may be designed to exert and to an extent disguise control or surveillance over the less developed country. This motive would become especially potent if the lesser country were to be nuclearized in the period before control responsibility fell to a major regional power or to an efficacious international organ. Finally, the alliance may have the object of projecting American influence by way of the less developed ally toward more aloof such countries. The possible intent of thus sponsoring a regional small-state association would realize most directly the third possible function of alliances—next to aggregation and control—that of concert.

To identify the less developed country or countries most suitable for politicomilitary alliance is comparable to identifying the less developed countries most promising as poles or pilots in economic development. It may be an even more delicate task. Although such a country must have solid reasons for seeking or accepting American alliance, and thus have an acute weak-

---

[2] The policy-oriented discussion in the balance of this section leans on a more basic analysis of alliances with respect to the less developed segment, to be published separately.

ness, the country ought also to have resources of inherent strength. Otherwise the country could not sustain the strains and derangements almost always attending an unequal and locally embattled alliance and still manifestly retain the key attributes of independence while in principle identifying with the imperial order without pursuing a local imperialism of its own. Unless an allied country does all of this, it cannot serve the purposes of American foreign and defense policies in any larger sense—as Pergamum, we may recall, was unable to serve Rome. It cannot, for instance, serve as a link with local small-state alignments from which the United States either keeps or is kept aloof, and it cannot serve with significant political effect as the locally respected ally liable to dampen the adverse features of what otherwise would be unilateral American intervention in a third country. Ultimate dependability combined with manifest independence in situations short of *casus foederis* is difficult to administer; more so than either dependence or integration, not least for the leading ally, and no less in the future in Asia or Africa than currently in Europe. While local prerequisites for dependable independence will be harder to come by in the less developed areas than in the North Atlantic area, the Afro-Asian parts of the world have the advantage of not laboring under the heritage of top-heavy organizational integration. The problem for the United States is one of locally suitable military hardware and mobile strategy at the shifting imperial frontier, but it is even more one of political manner, of the exercise of the economy of control as much as the economy of force.

To try to identify such dependably independent allies of the future in Africa today would be academic, and candidates in Latin America are as obvious as they are precarious. The more urgent need is in the more critical area, Asia. There, a South Korea may progressively meet most of the exacting requirements and assist the United States on a larger scale than, but on the model of, her token military contribution in Vietnam. The Philippines and Indonesia after Sukarno are other candidates, both favored and somewhat handicapped by being islands, just as Thailand is handicapped by being too directly exposed and too manifestly dependent, and Australia by being both an island and a dubiously Asian power. India is not literally a small power, but she is an undeveloped one. If she ever does move toward a responsible role in a South and Southeast Asian regional order, she is likely to shun the role of a preferred American ally regardless of the degree of her economic and technological dependence. Japan, finally, is neither small nor undeveloped; but, with the peculiar combination of strengths and weaknesses which make her into a kind of Asian Britain and Germany rolled in one, she might well pass through a phase of being America's Pergamum in the new and larger Asia. As of now, however, Japan is both a hesitant, regionally suspect, and economically not too solid candidate for a more active politicomilitary role vis-à-vis Communist China in particular. If she does allow herself to be activated by a likewise hesitant United States, moreover, Japan may well merely exchange her split political personality for another: she would have to stress political independence from the United States to appeal to Southeast Asians in quest of a new neutralism between America and China, while her continued and manifest tie-up with the United States would be necessary to secure the co-operation and assuage the fears of a South Korea or other key victims of Japan's imperialism, as the precondition for a progressive transfer of some of America's responsibilities in the area to Japan, perhaps by way of regional multilateral associations.

Multilateral associations or alliances of lesser states are something that the United States may find increasingly useful and feasible to sponsor or support, not least through the intermediary of an intimate local ally. The purposes of such associations can comprise such traditional functions of alliance as restraint over the more forward of the small-state allies or politicoeconomic consolidation in the face of a threatening or emerging regional great power (both of these purposes would be present in Indonesia's joining the Association of Southeast Asia consisting of Thailand, the Philippines, and Malaysia); moreover, as has been the case with the associations of politically "moderate" states in Africa, they can serve to superimpose an indigenous multilateral pattern over materially still more vital, bilateral alignments of members with the exmetropolitan or other greater powers. Small-state associations are no sure aggregators of strength; the problem is rather to prevent them from compounding the individual weaknesses of members. In this respect, it will be useful to keep in mind some of the failings of SEATO—such as the displacement of life-giving functions to other organizations, on the grounds of preventing "duplication"—and some of the tendencies of small-state associations in Africa—such as to stimulate ever new without consolidating existing associations, on the grounds of promoting "unity."

American influence ought to be employed to encourage fairly rapid development in such groupings or alliances of a substantial, if modest, core of military capability other than elaborate joint commands without rank and file, as the vital complement of politicoeconomic development and precondition of politically tolerable American military support in a crisis. More or less inclusive and effective associations—such as the Organization of African Unity and the Conseil de l'Entente in Africa, the Asian and Pacific Council and the Association of Southeast Asia—which shirk this requirement—if only because they seek to include too many heterogeneous elements, to offend no outside power, to reverse the traditional equation of alliance, and be for something and against no one—may do some good as initial tokens of increasing self-confidence and mutuality. But they can do harm if they indefinitely pre-empt the field, create a false impression of collective strength, and block or handicap smaller but tighter and more effective alignments. Only such alignments will prove on balance specifically useful to the United States as the discreet but decisive sponsor. That is to say, the possible liabilities implicit for a friendly great power in such associations—overinvolvement in local, interallied problems; danger of premature exclusion from the area in peace; and overly delayed re-entry under crisis conditions—will be outweighed by the advantages—such as meaningfully facilitated access to the area combined with a measure of controlled and reversible disengagement.

The military instrument continues to have key significance in the less developed segment. To accept this fact is not to deny that the preconditions of applying military force as well as conditions and attitudes surrounding actual military performance have changed.

The "preconditions" bear upon the modalities of access and control, while "performance" comprises commitment and intervention. Two main points may bear emphasis regarding access—the key word and concept distinguishing a multiregional imperial order.[3] One is that the requirements of political access will have to take increasing precedence over requirements of military logistics. In the many cases in which the two will be in conflict, the *mot d'ordre* will have to be indefinite access rather than permanent bases. Increasing mobility and decreasing dependence on a wide assortment of bases have been making this into a feasible requirement. To the real extent that an irreducible number of bases will continue to be essential, the importance of a few specially close allies will increase. As both the fully committed and indispensable allies and the rabid neutralists get fewer, political commitment and solidarity with regard to the indispensable ally will have to be reconciled with flexibility vis-à-vis other, not irreparably hostile, less developed countries. This will be made easier if an ultimately total political solidarity does not assume the mutually embarrassing forms of a military presence amounting to virtual occupation by the principal ally.

The second point to be made about access is less the kind of access than to whom access is to be available. To the extent that the distinction can be translated into implementing strategies, access should be increasingly to the lesser states for their own sakes rather than to the "real" great-power adversary by way of the lesser states, as was graphically the case with allies supplying facilities for the U2s. Capacity to protect against oppression by a locally imperialistic power must be freed, as much as possible, from the potential for provoking such power, however useful the "provocative" dispositions might be for ultimate protection

[3] See pp. 36–45 for definitions and illustrations.

against hypothetical dangers on a scale transcending the lesser power. If this requirement reduces the value of access for the United States from the viewpoint of total security, it will increase over time the feasibility of access in limited crises—which, for practical purposes, add up to total security most of the time.

The other precondition is that of control. Regarding kind, preference ought to be for indirect control, by way of the structure of local interests, over direct control, by way of either institutional integration or officious interference. For indirect control to be possible, self-interests of local actors must exist, be relatively stable in relation to one another, and be comprehensible to outsiders. A particularly awkward formative period may thus be unavoidable sooner or later, when external restraints are relaxed in order to facilitate the processes of interaction from which specific, stable, and comprehensible interests can emerge. The case for creative toleration of momentarily destructive conflicts among less developed countries relates to the question of "control for what purpose?" The object of control should be chiefly negative, in the sense of aiming to prevent extreme forms of behavior with more than local implications. One such extreme behavior is *under*-reaction to external threats from powers capable of vitally affecting the structure of access in the regional order and thus the global order; another is *over*reaction to local grievances, threats, ambitions, or provocations in conditions raising an immediate possibility of wider destabilization. In order to exert the necessary minimum of negative and indirect control, the United States must have at its command a military component capable of swaying the local balance of power and the equally manifest political will to employ that component. This brings up the problems of commitment and intervention as aspects of actual performance in an over-all imperial strategy.

The first question to raise about commitment is "for and against what?" The general answer for the immediate future is: For international order as a precisely envisaged, concrete distribution of power, responsibilities, and controls rather than vaguely envisaged state of peace; and against major threats to such order which, because major, are neither manageable by local resources nor likely to crystallize interests without abridging independence. The formulation implies that "international communism" is relegated to the status of one of a number of possible expansionist threats and that "world order" is more than a rationalization for anti-Communist acts and alliances. The commitment to uphold the bases of international order is apparently more sweeping than the commitment to contain the spearheads of international communism. It may seem to multiply tasks and create unnecessary enemies for the would-be global policeman. But the commitment is also reduced in scope if appropriately defined and managed in an international system in which the United States is not the sole, or sole countervailing, power of importance and with responsibility.

The reduction of scope can flow from at least two sources. First, it can flow from a strict, narrow interpretation of cases and situations activating the commitment; and it can flow, second, from an extensive conception of over-all or cumulative deterrence of disorder-generating acts by way of specific acts of defense or punishment. Despite ambiguities, it is generally possible to distinguish a conventional interstate conflict, revolving around territory and internation balance of power (such as that of India vs. Pakistan), from externally sponsored and supported internal coups and subversions (such as those in Yemen and Aden as well as in South Vietnam), aiming at domination or integral absorption. In the case of conventional inter-state conflicts, moreover, a distinction may be drawn between conflicts that are instigated or exploited by a potentially or actually dominant regional power and those that are not. An over-all American commitment to contain sources of international disorder might thus be limited to acts that risk to debase elementary standards of interstate behavior; to elevate an apparently expansionist power to a condition from which it could bar or impede future American access to a region; and acts that would terminate the relatively free, competitive–co-operative interaction among individual less developed countries as an essential condition of development. Where an intrinsically viable less developed country is confronted with superior power bent upon destroying or subjugating it, the United States should feel committed to play its part in "staying the hand" of the expansionist; where a locally legitimate conflict takes place over otherwise uncomposable differences, the commitment of the United States should be to no more than to "holding the ring" against exploitative outsiders and excessively acquisitive victors. Such national policy can be substantially consistent and impartial and can come to be widely accepted as being both. When this happens, the progressively established standards and precedents constitute a factor in cumulative deterrence of acts undermining both the existing international order and its potential for evolving toward regional autonomies and global concert; and the precedents may gain otherwise unavailable tolerance or support for analogous action in cases involving both "international" and "national" communism.

A firm answer, through consistent practice, to the

question concerning basic commitment "for and against what" enlarges the range of choice as to the specific form of commitment. It depends on the circumstances of a case whether the commitment is to be bilateral or multilateral; formal or informal; to a specified kind of military action or to support in general terms; mainly reassuring to the potential victim or threatening to the potential disturber. While informality and multilateralism have had a certain vogue, any attenuation of the anticolonial and neutralist psychoses will make it again possible to examine objectively the advantages and liabilities of particular forms of commitment. The choice may then be made in function of such things as timing and prospective efficacy. Timing may bear on the anticipated interval between commitment and actual eruption of acute crisis; efficacy will bear on fitness of alternative forms of commitment to maximize deterrence and facilitate advance planning for defensive or punitive action. To the extent that commitments are spelled out they may usefully be aimed against the employment of superior force rather than any force. In regard to roughly equal powers, this might mean commitment against simultaneous action by "two or more" powers, a formulation that covers the backing by a regionally major power of a small state proxy and that might be construed to cover backing by any regional state of insurgents in an internal war.

The greater the self-limitations that the United States accepts in regard to access, control, and basic commitment, moreover, the greater will rightfully both be and have to be its freedom concerning the kind of assistance or support to be rendered—the commitment "for what." Intimation or demonstration of general intent, naval or aerial, will suffice in some cases, as apparently did, for instance, the aerial demonstrations over Saudi Arabia in 1963 aimed to deter the United Arab Republic from extending its military action in Yemen to Saudi territory[4]; more direct involvement in hostilities will be necessary in other cases, such as in Santo Domingo at one end of the spectrum and in South Vietnam at the other. In either event, once it is implemented, commitment becomes direct intervention.

The specific kind of intervention will vary with controlling circumstances. One important aspect is the nature of the disturbance. In cases of disturbance comprising formally constituted states in a conflict of organized forces, it may suffice to suspend the conflict in order to deactivate the discord for all practical purposes, even without adjustment of substantive grievances. Whatever one may think of the bearing on international order of the imperative suspensions of the Anglo-French action in the Suez incident and of the Indo-Pakistani conflict over Kashmir, their aftermath would seem so far to warrant such a conclusion while also suggesting that necessities of government as well as the honor of states may still occasionally demand the use of force as a saving remedy or reprieve, regardless of outcome. When the disorder comprises disparate forces in a generalized melee or chaos, a deeper and more regulatory involvement may be necessary. Such would seem to have been the need in the Congo in the early 1960s. The Dominican situation a few years later—again apart from the question whether the American intervention or interposition was preventive in strictly local terms and then perhaps too precipitate or whether it was demonstrative of a larger intent and thus more opportune—falls somewhere between the two preceding types of disturbance. The sug-

[4] See *The New York Times,* June 13, 1966, p. 11.

gestive feature here is that the overt (and biased) nature of American military intervention imposed a responsibility on the United States to be equally active in securing a fair (and even inversely biased) political settlement, unlike what had been the case either for the covert United States intervention in Guatemala or for the multilateralized intervention under United Nations auspices in the Suez crisis in the 1950s.

If conceivable circumstances surrounding an intervention for this or that specific object are varied and complex, general precepts can be only few and ideally simple. They are basically two: maintain conspicuous capacity for intervention under the most varied conditions (the principle of "readiness") and combine such capacity with preference for locally inconspicuous intervention, when such intervention becomes mandatory (the principle of "scale"). Manifest capacity to intervene requires certain access to indispensable facilities in a crisis and, prior to crisis, demonstrative display of the ability to transfer striking power with all necessary speed. The inconspicuousness of actual intervention is enhanced, we have tried to suggest, whenever the United States enjoys the comfort of seconding, legitimizing, or at least in effect tolerant local governments. And, we must now add, an intervention will be least conspicuous in a military environment in which American assistance can be adjusted to the local scale of military capabilities and still promote its assigned purpose. To create such environment will require material assistance to less developed countries toward a respectable military capability; but it will also require the United States to employ military resources that do not vastly exceed locally available resources in technological sophistication and magnitude. Judging by the events in South Vietnam, great disparity between

American and local military resources would seem to accentuate momentum toward pre-emption of the conflict by United States forces and toward an employment of force that can be represented as inhuman, notably as regards the civilian population. (One possible example is the apparently reduced capacity for discriminating precision bombing on the part of planes flying too high and fast over areas of fighting.)

A deliberately "scaled" mode of intervention may well decrease military efficacy and increase American casualties, relative to combat methods employing the most sophisticated available weaponry with the greatest firepower. To the extent that this is true, two considerations apply. First of all, if a military intervention subject to the criterion of scale is expected to be less efficacious, it is more than ever essential that it take place before a serious deterioration in the fighting power of local forces has taken place. The worst approach would seem to be by way of a conspicuous commitment given far in advance of acute crisis and consequently subject to decay (a fair description of SEATO) and of a sizable assistance delayed too long to realize both efficacy and scale (a not unfair description of United States intervention in Vietnam). The exact opposite will often be preferable—that is to say, advance informal commitment combined with direct and specific warning, including intimation of contemplated action, to the adversary at the onset of acute crisis.

It will be also preferable to shift from defense to retributive sanction if the moment has passed when direct assistance scaled to fit the local resources can redress the imbalance. Retributive sanction employing massive air- or seapower against the principal accessible source of disturbance may not suffice effectively to defend the endangered less developed country; but it can nonetheless constitute a significant act in cumulative deterrence, heeded by potential disturbers, by raising the cost of whatever net gain may finally accrue to the punished party. The cost in civilian lives and economic resources, which the punitive strategy is likely to entail for the disturber, is matched by the political cost that the failure to defend entails for the punisher. Both must be assessed against two factors. One is the cost of belated, outscaled defense for the victim country; the other is the political cost for the United States of the cumulative effect on other countries of a policy under which defense tends to equal destruction—an impression that wore off somewhat in the years following the Korean war and has been revived and intensified in Vietnam. There is another consideration. If anything like a world order of graduated reciprocal access to individual regions for major powers does evolve, its over-all effect will be to inhibit and delay extraregional (meaning, in several regions, American) intervention in local conflicts comprising the regionally greater power or powers as the moderating or contending party. The involvement of a regional great power would enhance available local resources, thus relaxing for the United States the constraints of scale but also tending to make its military intervention subject to a relatively high level of violence. The manifest capacity and will to punish the originator of regional disturbance might then become even more essential than it is today, or even than would be the capacity and will to defend its object, if the United States as the foremost global power is to retain access to the region.

It is useful to distinguish between defense and retribution, scaled intervention and cumulative deterrence.

This is not to say, however, that the two strategies could not be combined in a concrete situation. In such a case, however, the exact mix is both crucial and controversial. In the Vietnamese conflict it is possible to identify as an error the decision to apply, at least initially, something close to the criterion of scale to the retributive aspect of the deterrent strategy, in a wrongful application of both the economy and the psychology of force, while discarding the principle of scale in the strictly defensive aspect of the combined operation.

The second consideration bears on the rate and level of American casualties under the employment of more or less sophisticated weaponry with greater or lesser firepower. It concerns the ultimately most vital single aspect of the role of the United States in regard to international order in the less developed segment. The United States cannot effectively implement global primacy (and thus prevent its passing into other hands or minimum international order being jeopardized in undeveloped areas) unless it manages to insulate its society and economy from traumatic impacts by each and every peripheral military involvement. One way to soften the impact of engagements in overseas conflicts would be a far-reaching professionalization of the military forces earmarked for such engagements. The character of such forces would facilitate timely intervention. The inevitably limited size of the forces would conform to the requirement of combining scale with efficacy; it would also determine the point at which defense on land would have to give way to (or be supplemented by) retribution from air or sea. If inflicted from behind the American nuclear-strategic shield and from the vantage point of an informed but relatively uninvolved public, both defense and retributive sanction might continue as long as necessary to achieve the desired political effect.

The financial costs and the political and moral dangers of increased reliance on professional soldiery for defense of remote frontiers are not negligible, even if the reliance is not complete and the legion is national rather than foreign. Nor can one ignore the traumas and liabilities consequent on acts of retribution, even if such acts implement cumulative deterrence of forcible assaults on national independence and international order. But all such costs must be weighed against the risks of social strains generated by recurrent communal overinvolvement in peripheral conflicts attending America's so-called overextension. The task is to avoid both pitfalls: initial overinvolvement and gradual lapse into civic indifference. The dilemma is a real one. It is of a kind that has been hardest to deal with for most or all willingly or unwillingly imperial—in the sense of order-maintaining—powers.

VIII. CONCLUSION

The Vietnamese war—the key relevant aspects of which have been summarized in the Preface—may well come to rank on a par with the two world wars as a conflict that marked an epoch in America's progress toward definition of her role as a world power. It will even more certainly be coupled in retrospect with the different but comparable as well as coincident ordeal of American adjustment in Europe to the consequences of the victories in World War II and that war's extension into the cold war. If the United States comes out of the military confrontation in Asia and out of the diplomatic confrontation in Europe with a sharpened sense of how to differentiate its role and distribute the various components of national power in the different areas of the world, it will have ascended to the crucial and perhaps last step toward the plateau of maturity. It will then have fulfilled the early hopes of its spiritual or actual founders and will have become a true empire —a strong and salient power with the sense of a task exceeding its national limits but not its national resources.

To sustain the most difficult of political roles in a far from favorable political climate without failings is beyond human possibility. To undertake it at all seriously in a sustained rather than fitful manner may be beyond the capacity of contemporary Americans. They strike the onlooker as a breed of men who, if they possess in sufficient measure the swashbuckling spirit of the pioneering frontiersman or crusading conquistador in conditions of overt conflict, are singularly unprepared and even unfitted by the prevailing values of their domestic existence for the role of proconsuls, who are required to display unassailable self-assurance in ambiguous situations of muted hostility or highly conditional and qualified friendship. It is not enough to disinter for the American public the exemplar of imperial Rome in mass circulation magazines and popular television programs. Nor is it, of course, necessary to replicate in the midst of a mass society the mythical paragons of individual and collective Roman virtues. The hiatus between the early vision of empire in this country and its accomplishment on the global stage has been too great in terms of both time and dominant social profile. Moreover, the United States has not had the benefit of gradually ascending to empire by at least half-deliberate choice and an ever more wholehearted effort, however much the outward outlines of America's expansion may parallel those of Rome.

The task of this country is, fortunately, more limited than was that of Rome. The United States is not the sole major power in the relevant world, even if it is the primary power; and the peace, construed as absence of major war, which it is to supervise is not only an American, but also and perhaps primarily a nuclear, peace, even if on the subnuclear level the world order may have to be to a large extent an American order. And, perhaps most importantly, on the strength of a combination of political ideals and economic realities, the United States can hope to exert an imperial role with greater magnanimity than the Romans were either prepared for or even able to exercise. The greatest test for the display of such magnanimity is now in America's Greece, Europe; the most grueling test of resolution in creating the preconditions of magnanimity is apt to be, as it was for Rome, in Asia. Together, Europe and Asia still add up to the inner core of the *orbis terrarum*. Together, resolution and magnanimity still constitute the essence of *imperium*.

A great strain on American foreign policy will henceforth originate in the need to administer the disparity between Europe and Afro-Asia in the face of pressures and demands to retain controls in Europe—as if she were in the inchoate state and, at best, formative stage of today's Afro-Asia—or to relax involvements in Afro-Asia—as if she already matched Europe's possession of the makings of a balance of power. Any substantial relaxing of American politico-diplomatic and military hegemony in Europe will be opposed as a prelude to intensified conflicts among West Europeans, which, exploited by the Soviet Union, will compel the United States to reinvolve itself politically and militarily under the most adverse conditions. This argument will ignore or minimize the built-in safeguards against such a consequence of disengagement, due to a largely self-equilibrating new structure of material power and political interests within and outside Europe. On the other hand, the relaxing of American military and direct political involvements in Afro-Asia will be urged as the necessary prelude to revealing and intensifying latent conflicts among local powers—notably between China and lesser, Communist or non-Communist, powers—which, properly exploited by the United States, will enable it to reduce American engagement and implement the residual one more effectively. This argument will minimize or ignore the impediment to such a felicitous dynamic due to the psychopolitical tendency in Afro-Asia toward cumulatively disequilibrating (or, stampeding) response to any but the most conspicuously and (for local elites) safely manageable greater-power expansionist pressure.

The diffusion of greater conventional power to lesser and yet undeveloped states is no less desirable—though less controversially so—than the diffusion of nuclear power to major industrial states, in the interest of a progressive restoration of a multiregional, global balance of power system on all levels of conflict and potential order (or disorder). But a balanced diffusion of power, conventional or nuclear, is not something to be postulated in an "as if" type of striking analysis; it is something to outline painstakingly in partially self-contradictory analysis and manage in like action over a long period of time. Projections cannot guide policies if they overleap the intermediate, short-term processes for arriving at the desired state. Self-consciously to manage multipolarization and its political implications in and for Afro-Asia—as the United States unconsciously, unwittingly, and, it sometimes appears, unwillingly did in Europe—is the ingrate role for an imperially "overinvolved" America in the context of what bids fair to remain for some time yet a unifocal international system of at best complementary imbalances. It would be as misleading to view and conduct international politics on the basis of anticipated and partially simulated multipolarity on global scale as it was distorting to view and conduct the cold war on the basis of anticipated and partially simulated parity between the two world powers—notwithstanding the difference that multipolarity may come to be widely desired on the basis of common sense in most respects except the nuclear one, while superpower parity came to be regarded as desirable only in nuclear terms on the basis of specialized theory of strategic stability.

An imperial policy for the U.S. will thus have to fight off two kinds of intellectual and political opposition. One, vocal and widely held, opposition will stress a posited imbalance between global objectives and national resources, implying a deficiency of American power and resource in the present; another, perhaps increasing and more subtle, analysis will posit the potential existence of balances of power and conflicts of interest among foreign states, implying the capacity for American policy to activate them by dint of masterful inactivity in areas of controversial immediate strategic significance. A good possibility is, however, that only a policy incurring the charge of imbalance of national means and imperial ends can move us closer in the foreseeable future to the reality of a largely autonomous balance of power and pragmatic interests internationally, always with the proviso that the creations of American involvement of today will become hard-to-control contenders of tomorrow and potential adversaries in the conflict of the day after tomorrow.

If the necessity for embattled great powers to aid in promoting present allies to independent actors and potential adversaries in future conflicts is one of the few established laws of international history, it is a matter of historic justice that the United States— having benefited by conflicts among stronger European states while fulfilling its "manifest destiny" of independence and continental expansion—should now assume some of the burdens of conflicts involving other powers, including those that concern her only indirectly and even disputably. There is little ground for self-pity. If physical distance from reciprocally stalemated power centers conferred on the United States an immunity to disastrous consequence of miscalculation of power and interests in the phase of its continental expansion, its economic capacity for outdistancing others in the magnitude of national power has largely preserved that immunity for this country in the period of involvement in a global system with few but psychological and policy-induced "distances" among nations. And there is little margin for radical self-retrenchment. The transiency of mood which brought to a halt America's leap into overseas imperialism at the turn of the century is unlikely to affect likewise America's imperial function in the second half. An exuberant policy of external interference and expansion, born of a mood, can fade with the next change in mood; a policy of leadership for a balance of power-to-be, rooted in a configuration of forces and pressures, however, can pass away only with that configuration. An adverse turn in the national mood of an imperial community can terminate the imperial task prematurely only by accelerating the decline and decay of the community itself both as international actor and as national body politic.

The function defining great nations—and constituting their manifest destiny—has always been first, to consolidate a viable habitat to the outermost natural and morally sanctionable limits; and, secondly, having done so and outgrown the adolescent oscillations in moods between exuberance and seclusion, to contribute in their maturity to the construction and consolidation of a wider matrix of order. Such order serves more than one purpose. It is the stage for self-affirmation in the time of strength and vigor; it is the creator's support in moments of failing and, for a time, in his eventual decline in strength relative to others. And, last but not least, it is a feat to be remembered, and a model to be imitated, after the imperial creator has left the world of action for the realm of history.

SELECTED BIBLIOGRAPHY

Bozeman, Adda, *Politics and Culture in International History* (Princeton: 1960).

Braudel, François, *La Méditerranée et le monde méditerranéen à l'époque de Philippe II* (Paris: 1949).

Brzezinski, Zbigniew, *Alternative to Partition* (New York: 1965).

Frank, Tenney, *Roman Imperialism* (New York: 1921).

Hassner, Pierre and John Newhouse, *Diplomacy in the West* (New York: 1966).

Heuss, Alfred, "Das Zeitalter der Revolution," in Golo Mann and Alfred Heuss (eds.), *Propyläen Weltgeschichte,* Vol. IV (Berlin: 1963).

Hoffmann, Stanley, "Obstinate or Obsolete? The Fate of the Nation-State and the Case of Western Europe," *Daedalus* (1966).

Hoffmann, Wilhelm, "Roms Aufstieg zur Weltherrschaft," *Propyläen Weltgeschichte,* Vol. IV (Berlin: 1963).

Layton, Christopher, *Trans-Atlantic Investments* (Boulogne-sur-Seine: 1966).

Liska, George, *Europe Ascendant* (Baltimore: 1964).

——, *Nations in Alliance* (Baltimore: 1962).

——, "Nuclear Diffusion: Domestic, Regional, and Global Perspectives," in Alden Williams (ed.), *Arms, Science, and Politics* (Columbus, Ohio: forthcoming).

Masters, Roger D., *The Nation Is Burdened* (New York: 1967).

Modelski, George (ed.), *SEATO* (Canberra: 1962).

Morley, James W., *Japan and Korea* (New York: 1965).

Oppenheim, A. Leo, *Ancient Mesopotamia* (Chicago: 1964).

Pirenne, Jacques, *Histoire de la civilisation de l'Egypte ancienne* (2 vols.; Neuchâtel: 1961–63).

————, *The Tides of History,* Vol. I (London: 1963).

Stoessinger, John G., *The United Nations and the Superpowers* (New York: 1965).

Strauch, Hanspeter F., *Panafrika* (Zurich: 1964).

Thiam, Doudou, *The Foreign Policy of African States* (London: 1965).

Toynbee, Arnold J., *Hellenism* (New York: 1959).

Uru, Jon, *La politique orientale de François I* (Paris: 1908).

Welles, C. Brandford, "Die hellenistische Welt," *Propyläen Weltgeschichte,* Vol. III (Berlin: 1962).

Zartman, I. William, "Characteristics of Developing Foreign Policies," in William H. Lewis (ed.), *French-Speaking Africa* (New York: 1965).